QA Testing Book

"A Pro-Level Guide to Advanced Risk Management and Quality Strategies"

Kevin Reyes

© **Copyright 2023 - All rights reserved.**

The contents of this book may not be reproduced, duplicated or transmitted without direct written permission from the author.

Under no circumstances will any legal responsibility or blame be held against the publisher for any reparation, damages, or monetary loss due to the information herein, either directly or indirectly.

Legal Notice:
This book is copyright protected. This is only for personal use. You cannot amend, dis-tribute, sell, use, quote or paraphrase any part or the content within this book without the consent of the author.

Disclaimer Notice:
Please note the information contained within this document is for educational and entertainment purposes only. Every attempt has been made to provide accurate, up to date and reliable complete information. Readers acknowledge that the author is not engaging in the rendering of legal, financial, medical or professional advice. The content of this book has been derived from various sources. Please consult a licensed professional before attempting any techniques outlined in this book.

By reading this document, the reader agrees that under no circumstances is the author responsible for any losses, direct or indirect, which are incurred as a result of the use of information contained within this document.

Table of Contents

Introduction 4

Chapter One: Advanced Concepts in Quality Assurance 19

Chapter Two: Risk Management Fundamentals 31

Chapter Three: Implementing Risk Management Strategies . 41

Chapter Four: Quality Metrics and Analysis 51

Chapter Five: Cost Management in QA 62

Chapter Six: Resource Allocation and Optimization 74

Chapter Seven: Advanced Test Design Techniques 86

Chapter Eight: High-Level Test Automation Strategy 96

Chapter Nine: Continuous Improvement Processes 108

Chapter Ten: Change Management in QA 121

Chapter Eleven: Quality Assurance Leadership 132

Chapter Twelve: Compliance and Standards 142

Chapter Thirteen: Advanced Security Testing 153

Chapter Fourteen: Future Trends in QA 165

Chapter Fifteen: Case Studies and Real-World Applications. 176

Conclusion 189

Introduction

Summary of Intermediate Knowledge

As Quality Assurance (QA) professionals progress from basic to intermediate levels, they build upon foundational knowledge to embrace more intricate tools and methodologies. This transition is crucial for effectively handling sophisticated QA tasks and leveraging high-level automation techniques that boost both the efficacy and thoroughness of testing processes. This summary explores key intermediate concepts, tools, and methods essential for any QA professional looking to elevate their career.

Proficiency with Automation Tools and Frameworks

Intermediate QA practitioners should have robust experience with a range of automation tools and frameworks that simplify and enhance the testing process. For example, Selenium WebDriver is crucial for automating browser interactions, allowing testers to execute commands across different browsers to test web applications. Similarly, tools like Postman facilitate API testing by sending requests to web services and analyzing responses efficiently.

Below is a Python script demonstrating how to use Selenium WebDriver to check a web page's title:

```python
from selenium import webdriver

# Start the Chrome Driver
driver = webdriver.Chrome()

# Visit the website
driver.get("https://www.example.com")

# Verify the title is as expected
assert "Example Domain" in driver.title

# End the browser session
driver.quit()
```

Understanding frameworks such as TestNG or JUnit is also critical, as they enable organized, scalable, and manageable testing through features like test grouping, annotations, and sequential execution.

Programming and Scripting Skills

Knowledge of programming languages, notably Python or Java, is crucial at this stage. Intermediate expertise involves not just basic scripting but also a deeper understanding of data structures, object-oriented principles, and sophisticated error handling, which are indispensable for crafting complex automation scripts and managing runtime exceptions.

Here's how exception handling might appear in a Java-based test script:

```java
try {
    // Attempt to interact with an element
    driver.findElement(By.id("nonexistent-element")).click();
} catch (NoSuchElementException e) {
    System.out.println("Element not found: " + e.getMessage());
} finally {
    driver.quit();
}
```

CI/CD Pipeline Integration

An intermediate QA specialist must be adept at integrating testing protocols within Continuous Integration/Continuous Deployment (CI/CD) pipelines. Utilizing tools like Jenkins, GitLab CI, or CircleCI automates the testing process, ensuring that code merges are validated and that the application remains stable and deployable at any point.

An example of a Jenkins pipeline script might include:

```groovy
pipeline {
    agent any
    stages {
        stage('Build') {
            steps {
                // Compile the application
                sh 'make build'
            }
        }
        stage('Test') {
            steps {
                // Execute automated tests
                sh 'make test'
            }
        }
        stage('Deploy') {
            steps {
                // Deploy the application to production
                sh 'make deploy'
            }
        }
    }
}
```

Understanding Advanced Testing Techniques

Knowledge in performance and load testing is also critical at this level, with tools like JMeter or LoadRunner used to simulate high traffic and analyze the application's performance under stress.

Security Testing Insights

Security becomes a more prominent focus at the intermediate level. Understanding threats such as SQL injections, XSS, and security misconfigurations is essential. Security testing tools like OWASP ZAP help automate the discovery of vulnerabilities.

Utilizing OWASP ZAP via its API for security testing could be exemplified as follows:

```
from zapv2 import ZAPv2

# Initialize connection to ZAP instance
zap = ZAPv2(apikey='your-api-key')

# Start scanning the target site
scan_id = zap.spider.scan('http://example.com')

# Ensure the scan completes
while (int(zap.spider.status(scan_id)) < 100) {
    time.sleep(2)

# Begin active scanning for vulnerabilities
zap.ascan.scan('http://example.com')
```

Conclusion

Broadening one's scope from basic to intermediate QA entails a deep dive into complex tools and methodologies that are integral for high-quality software development. This stage is vital for professionals poised to take on greater challenges, offering the tools and knowledge necessary to spearhead advanced QA initiatives and leadership roles within the industry.

The Importance of Risk Management in QA

In today's tech-driven environment, Quality Assurance (QA) plays an essential role in ensuring software not only complies with technical specifications but also meets user demands and adheres to legal standards. At the heart of effective QA lies risk management, a methodological process aimed at identifying, analyzing, and mitigating risks that could detrimentally impact software quality. This process is paramount not just for safeguarding the product's performance but also for directing QA efforts strategically towards areas posing the greatest risk. This overview emphasizes the critical nature of risk management in QA and its influential role in guiding software project outcomes.

Identification and Prioritization of Risks

Risk management starts with pinpointing potential hazards that range from minor user interface issues to severe security vulnerabilities that could jeopardize the entire system. Post identification, these risks undergo a thorough assessment regarding their potential impact and probability of occurrence, which is essential for their prioritization. This step enables QA teams to allocate their resources effectively, focusing on the most critical aspects first.

For example, consider a software application designed for banking transactions. A risk assessment might reveal that flaws in transaction security pose a high risk due to their potential for severe financial implications and the relatively high chance of such issues arising. Identifying these risks early helps ensure that significant resources are dedicated to testing and securing this crucial functionality.

Effective Risk Assessment Methods

To assess risks efficiently, several proven techniques are employed. The Risk Matrix, for instance, visually maps out risks by categorizing them according to the severity of impact and likelihood of occurrence, facilitating straightforward prioritization. Another systematic approach is the Failure Modes and Effects Analysis (FMEA), which focuses on identifying potential failure points in software. An example of applying FMEA to a software module might include:

1. **Identification**: Cataloging potential failures, such as inaccuracies in a user data processing module.

2. **Analysis**: Assigning severity, occurrence, and detection ratings. For instance, errors in data processing might receive a high severity rating due to potential data breaches.

3. **Prioritization**: Computing a Risk Priority Number (RPN) by multiplying the given ratings, where higher RPNs indicate a pressing need for immediate intervention.

Strategies for Risk Mitigation

Following risk assessment, formulating and implementing risk mitigation strategies is crucial. This could involve modifications to the software design, enhancement of testing procedures, or improved error handling protocols. For instance, to mitigate risks in user data processing, more robust data validation checks might be integrated:

```python
def check_user_data(user_data):
    if not validate_user_data_format(user_data):
        raise ValueError("Data format incorrect")
    if not user_data_is_secure(user_data):
        raise SecurityError("Data security validation failed")
    return True
```

Moreover, continuous monitoring of risks is facilitated by automated testing and integration tools like Jenkins or Travis CI, which ensure that any newly introduced risks are promptly detected and addressed.

Cultural Influence of Risk Management

Risk management also significantly influences organizational culture by promoting an anticipatory approach to quality. It encourages a proactive attitude where quality is seen as a collective responsibility, motivating team members to remain vigilant about potential risks and their possible repercussions. This proactive stance not only enhances the product quality but also boosts team morale and operational efficiency by minimizing the occurrence of unexpected issues during later stages of the project.

Conclusion

In conclusion, risk management is foundational to effective QA strategies. It involves a strategic and thorough approach to identifying, analyzing, and mitigating risks, ensuring that software not only functions as intended but also remains secure and reliable. By embedding risk management practices within QA processes, organizations can prevent major failures, optimize resource utilization, and deliver superior products. The role of risk management in QA is therefore indispensable, ensuring that software projects are successfully delivered while maintaining the integrity of the business and its offerings.

Objectives of This Book

The domain of Quality Assurance (QA) continually shifts and expands, necessitating ongoing professional development and strategic adaptability from those engaged in its practice. "A Pro-Level Guide to Advanced Risk Management and Quality Strategies" is crafted to offer seasoned QA professionals a deep dive into the advanced aspects of risk management and quality assurance. This guide aims to equip readers with the knowledge and tools required to effectively manage complex software projects and to lead QA teams towards successful project completions.

1. Advancing Understanding of Sophisticated QA Concepts

This book intends to expand the reader's grasp of complex QA theories and practices, advancing them from intermediate levels to expert mastery. It covers the integration of comprehensive QA strategies within software development workflows and elucidates advanced topics such as Quantitative Risk Analysis (QRA). For instance, a basic example of implementing QRA in Python is shown below:

```python
# Illustration of Quantitative Risk Analysis (QRA) calculation
def calculate_risk_probability(impact, likelihood):
    return impact * likelihood

# Assign impact and likelihood values
impact = 0.7  # 70% impact on project outcomes
likelihood = 0.5  # 50% probability of occurrence

# Execute risk probability calculation
risk_probability = calculate_risk_probability(impact, likelihood)
print(f"Risk probability: {risk_probability}")
```

2. Arming Readers with Tools for Advanced Risk Management

With the increasing complexity of software projects, managing associated risks effectively is critical. This book provides detailed insights into developing strategies for risk mitigation, transferring risks, and devising comprehensive management plans. Through real-world case studies and examples, readers will learn how to apply these strategies effectively in various scenarios.

3. Deepening Knowledge of Quality Metrics and Analytical Techniques

The effective use of quality metrics is essential for assessing and improving QA processes. This book aims to enhance readers' understanding of advanced metrics that measure software quality and provides strategies for employing these metrics to make informed decisions. Discussions will include how to calculate and interpret metrics like the Defect Leakage Ratio and Automation ROI.

4. Exploring Advanced Test Automation Strategies

Automation is fundamental to modern QA processes. This book explores in-depth test automation strategies, focusing on selecting and implementing enterprise-level tools and frameworks that integrate with DevOps practices. It also addresses the newest technologies in automation, aiding readers in selecting the best tools for their organizational needs.

Here's an example of how tool selection might be approached programmatically:

```python
# Function to select an automation tool based on defined criteria

def select_automation_tool(tools, criteria):
    suitable_tools = [tool for tool in tools if tool['performance'] >=
        criteria['performance'] and
                      tool['usability'] >= criteria['usability']]
    return suitable_tools

# Define tools and criteria
available_tools = [
    {'name': 'Tool A', 'performance': 85, 'usability': 75},
    {'name': 'Tool B', 'performance': 80, 'usability': 80},
    {'name': 'Tool C', 'performance': 90, 'usability': 70}
]
criteria = {'performance': 80, 'usability': 75}

# Apply selection function
selected_tools = select_automation_tool(available_tools, criteria)
print(f"Tools selected: {[tool['name'] for tool in selected_tools]}")
```

5. Preparing QA Professionals for Leadership

Finally, this book prepares QA professionals for leadership by discussing essential skills beyond the technical—such as strategic planning, decision-making, and effective communication. These sections are designed to prepare readers for senior-level responsibilities within their organizations.

Conclusion

By fulfilling these objectives, "A Pro-Level Guide to Advanced Risk Management and Quality Strategies" not only seeks to enhance the current capabilities of QA professionals but also to prepare them for upcoming challenges and leadership roles within the dynamic landscape of Quality Assurance.

Guide to Maximizing Benefit from This Book

As Quality Assurance (QA) professionals strive to keep pace with the rapid advancements and transformations in the tech landscape, ongoing learning and practical application of new knowledge are paramount. "A Pro-Level Guide to Advanced Risk Management and Quality Strategies" offers an in-depth exploration into sophisticated risk management and quality assurance tactics. Here, we provide a comprehensive approach on how to effectively engage with this resource to enhance your professional skills and apply these insights into your everyday QA tasks.

1. Deliberate Reading and Application

To fully benefit from this book, a deliberate and structured approach to reading and application is recommended:

- **Review and Reinforce**: Begin by going through chapters that cover familiar ground to reinforce your existing understanding, which will provide a solid foundation for tackling more complex topics.

- **Progress Sequentially**: Follow the book in the order presented. Each chapter is designed to build on the previous one, layering knowledge in a way that enhances comprehension of more intricate subjects as you progress.

- **Hands-On Implementation**: Apply the concepts practically as you learn them. For instance, if a chapter discusses a new testing framework, try setting it up and running some test cases. This direct application will help solidify your understanding and give you confidence in using new tools.

An example might include a simple Python script to test basic automation functionality:

```python
# Simple Python script to test web page automation

def check_page_title(url, expected_title):
    from selenium import webdriver
    driver = webdriver.Chrome()
    driver.get(url)
    assert expected_title in driver.title
    driver.close()

# Example usage of the function
check_page_title('http://example.com/login', 'Expected Login Page')
```

2. Leverage Supplementary Resources

Maximize learning by fully engaging with the supplementary materials provided in the book:

- **Study Case Studies**: Deep dive into the case studies that illustrate practical applications of theoretical knowledge. Analyze them to understand their implications and adapt these strategies to suit your own QA scenarios.

- **Use Downloadable Tools**: Apply the downloadable checklists, templates, and tools provided in the book to real projects. These resources are crafted to be used directly in professional settings.

- **Explore Linked Resources**: For chapters that include links to external resources, ensure you visit these sites to expand your understanding and keep abreast of current trends.

3. Direct Application to Current Projects

Implement what you learn immediately into your current projects:

- **Integration Into Workflows**: As new strategies and tools are introduced, integrate them into your existing projects. This real-time application helps bridge the gap between theoretical knowledge and practical use.

- **Create a Feedback Loop**: Establish a systematic approach to evaluate the effectiveness of new techniques. Feedback from these evaluations will guide continuous improvement and help refine your QA processes.

4. Engage with the QA Community

The learning process can be greatly enhanced by active participation in the QA community:

- **Engage in Discussions**: Participate in online forums and discussions. These interactions can provide new insights and alternative approaches to common challenges.

- **Network at Events**: Attend relevant QA and tech conferences. Networking with peers and industry leaders can provide further depth to the concepts discussed in the book.

5. Reflect and Revisit Regularly

Maintain a routine of revisiting the material and reflecting on your learnings:

- **Periodic Review**: Regularly go back to the book to refresh your knowledge and stay aligned with best practices.
- **Document Learning Outcomes**: Consider keeping a journal of how the book's content has been applied in your projects and the outcomes thereof.

Conclusion

Achieving maximum benefit from "A Pro-Level Guide to Advanced Risk Management and Quality Strategies" involves more than passive reading. It requires active engagement with the material, practical application of the concepts, and a commitment to continuous learning and community involvement. By following this comprehensive approach, you can ensure that you fully utilize the book to advance your QA capabilities and effectively lead your teams and projects.

Chapter One

Advanced Concepts in Quality Assurance

Defining Quality at a Strategic Level

Quality Assurance (QA) in the context of strategic management transcends routine testing to become an integral part of an organization's overarching goals, directly affecting customer satisfaction and market position. This exploration delves into the strategic definition of quality, illustrating how it can be seamlessly incorporated into the operational framework of an organization to drive comprehensive business success.

Strategic Quality Management Explained

At its core, strategic quality management involves embedding quality objectives within the fabric of an organization's vision and operational strategies. This ensures that quality assurance is not just a checkbox in the QA department but a critical organizational priority that influences all functional areas. By strategically managing quality, businesses set benchmarks that all products, services, and processes must meet or exceed, thereby ensuring customer satisfaction and fostering business growth.

Utilizing Established Frameworks and Standards

To systematize their approach to quality, many organizations turn to established frameworks such as ISO 9001, Six Sigma, or Total Quality Management (TQM). These frameworks provide a robust structure for defining, measuring, and achieving quality goals that align with strategic business objectives.

For instance, adopting ISO 9001 typically involves the creation of a quality management system (QMS) that highlights several key areas:

- **Customer Focus**: Making customer requirements a primary focus.

- **Leadership Vision**: Promoting a unified direction within the leadership team.

- **Engagement of People**: Ensuring that all levels of the organization are engaged in the QMS.

- **Process Approach**: Treating activities as processes that contribute to a linked system.

- **Continual Improvement**: Committing to ongoing improvements across the organization.

- **Evidence-based Decision Making**: Using data to inform decision-making.

- **Relationship Management**: Optimizing performance by managing relationships with all stakeholders.

These components are adaptable to the specific strategic needs of any organization, fostering a pervasive quality-centric culture.

Setting Strategic Quality Metrics

At the strategic level, defining specific quality metrics is crucial. These metrics provide essential data that helps to steer decision-making and evaluate the effectiveness of quality initiatives. Metrics might include customer satisfaction rates, defect frequencies, coverage metrics in testing, or efficiency metrics in production.

For example, 'Mean Time to Failure' (MTTF) is a metric used in software development to measure product reliability:

```python
# Python code to calculate Mean Time to Failure (MTTF)
def calculate_mttf(total_operational_hours, number_of_failures):
    if number_of_failures == 0:
        return float('inf')  # Indicates perfect reliability
    return total_operational_hours / number_of_failures

# Example MTTF calculation
operational_hours = 15000  # Total operational hours
failures = 20  # Total observed failures
mttf = calculate_mttf(operational_hours, failures)
print(f"Mean Time to Failure: {mttf} hours")
```

This metric is vital for assessing the average time between failures, providing insights into the reliability of the software product.

Ensuring Alignment with Business Goals

Quality at a strategic level must dovetail with broader business objectives, such as increasing market share, improving customer retention, or enhancing brand reputation. Thus, quality goals are crafted not just for compliance but as fundamental contributors to business performance and customer loyalty, requiring periodic reassessment to align with market feedback and technological advancements.

Promoting a Quality-Driven Culture

Clear and consistent communication from leadership is essential in promoting a culture that values quality. Strategic quality management depends on conveying the importance of quality in achieving business success and clarifying the role of each team member in this endeavor. This approach helps cultivate an environment where quality is seen as a collective responsibility and a key driver of organizational success.

Conclusion

Strategically defining and managing quality involves a holistic approach that integrates leadership commitment, cultural adaptation, and operational execution, with a focus on continuous improvement and customer alignment. By defining quality at a strategic level, organizations ensure that their QA measures are not only effective for immediate needs but also instrumental in driving long-term business growth and maintaining a strong competitive stance in their industry.

Quality Assurance vs. Quality Control

In modern product development and management, Quality Assurance (QA) and Quality Control (QC) are pivotal concepts, often confused or used interchangeably. However, these terms represent fundamentally different approaches within the quality management framework. Their distinct roles are crucial for organizations striving to enhance product quality and fulfill consumer expectations efficiently. This analysis will define QA and QC, differentiate their objectives, and illustrate their application within a robust quality strategy.

Quality Assurance: Emphasizing Process Optimization

Quality Assurance encompasses the methodologies and activities aimed at ensuring the consistent achievement of quality requirements. QA is inherently process-oriented, focusing on preventing defects by enhancing the processes involved in product or service development. This approach includes a variety of proactive measures such as system audits, compliance checks, and process improvements, all designed to prevent issues before they arise.

The essence of QA lies in creating a reliable system that instills confidence in an organization's ability to deliver high-quality products or services consistently. It involves structured activities such as staff training, procedural documentation, and routine process assessments to ensure operational efficiency and effectiveness.

Consider a software development team that employs QA practices incorporating regular code reviews and automated testing within their workflows to identify and resolve issues promptly. Below is an example of how automated testing might be integrated:

```python
# Example Python script for automated unit testing using PyTest

def multiply(x, y):
    return x * y

def test_multiply():
    assert multiply(2, 3) == 6
    assert multiply('a', 3) == 'aaa'  # This test will fail, showcasing how bugs
        are caught early.

# This script can be executed using a command-line tool to automatically run the
    test_multiply function
```

Quality Control: Focused on Product Integrity

In contrast, Quality Control is concerned with the identification of defects in the final products. QC is product-oriented, involving operational techniques and activities that fulfill quality standards by detecting flaws in finished products. It is a reactive process that assumes defects will occur and aims to identify these defects before the products reach the consumer.

QC typically involves practical tasks such as inspections, testing, and measurements to ensure that products do not deviate from the defined quality specifications. This function is often carried out by specialized QC personnel who operate independently from production teams to maintain objectivity.

For instance, in manufacturing, QC might involve testing samples from production batches against predefined quality criteria. Products that fail to meet these standards may be rejected or returned for corrections, ensuring that only compliant products are delivered to the market.

Synergizing QA and QC

Although QA and QC serve different purposes, they complement each other and are both essential for a comprehensive quality management system. Improvements made through QA processes can minimize the occurrence of defects, thereby reducing the burden on QC to catch these defects. Conversely, insights gained from QC activities can inform QA processes, highlighting areas for enhancement.

An example of how QA and QC can be integrated in software development involves the use of continuous integration (CI) tools that automate testing and results reporting. Here's how such a setup might look:

```
# Example configuration for a CI tool like Jenkins to automate tests
pipeline {
    agent any
    stages {
        stage('Build') {
            steps {
                sh 'make build'
            }
        }
        stage('Test') {
            steps {
                sh 'pytest tests/'
            }
        }
        stage('Deploy') {
            steps {
                sh 'make deploy'
            }
        }
    }
    post {
        always {
            archiveArtifacts artifacts: '*.log', fingerprint: true
            junit '**/test-reports/*.xml'
        }
    }
}
```

Conclusion

To summarize, Quality Assurance and Quality Control, though often conflated, play distinct yet complementary roles in the pursuit of product excellence. QA focuses on enhancing processes to prevent defects, while QC aims to detect defects in final products. Together, they form an integral part of a strategic approach to quality management, ensuring both product reliability and consumer satisfaction. For any organization committed to quality, understanding and effectively implementing both QA and QC is vital for achieving outstanding product standards and maintaining competitive edge in their respective markets.

Establishing Quality Goals for Enterprise

In today's fast-paced market environment, setting clear and measurable quality goals is paramount for enterprises striving to enhance their competitive stance and ensure customer satisfaction. These goals serve as critical indicators for directing improvements in product and service standards, optimizing operational efficiencies, and enhancing customer interactions. It's essential for these goals to be SMART—specific, measurable, achievable, relevant, and time-bound—to effectively guide the company's efforts towards achieving quality excellence. This narrative outlines the process for establishing such goals, integrating strategic insights and effective implementation strategies to foster a strong quality-oriented culture within an organization.

Importance of Quality Goals in Business Strategy

Quality goals are central to an organization's strategic quality management, acting as guiding beacons for ongoing organizational improvements. Aligning these goals with wider business objectives ensures a concerted effort across all departments, moving in harmony towards enhanced quality standards. Defined with precision, these goals facilitate efficient resource management, target key performance improvements, and enable measurable tracking of progress.

Defining Effective Quality Goals

To drive significant advancements, quality goals should encapsulate the following attributes:

- **Specific**: Defined with clarity to ensure focus and comprehensibility across the organization.

- **Measurable**: Established with quantifiable criteria to track progress and validate achievements.

- **Achievable**: Set within realistic bounds, considering available resources, to foster attainable successes.

- **Relevant**: Tightly linked to both strategic business objectives and customer needs to ensure impactful contributions.

- **Time-bound**: Framed within a specific timeline to promote prompt action and enable regular reviews.

Example of a SMART Quality Goal

Consider a hypothetical goal in a telecommunications company: "Enhance call quality by reducing dropped calls by 30% within the next year through network upgrades and optimizing routing algorithms." This goal is specific (focuses on call quality), measurable (30% reduction), achievable (through technological enhancements), relevant (improves customer experience), and time-bound (one-year target).

Strategic Aspects in Setting Quality Goals

When crafting quality goals, several strategic considerations should be evaluated:

- **Customer Insights**: Understanding customer priorities helps ensure that quality improvements align with market demands.

- **Benchmarking Industry Standards**: Keeping pace with industry benchmarks and competitor performance guarantees that quality goals are ambitious yet attainable.

- **Compliance with Regulations**: Aligning goals with regulatory standards is crucial for legal operations and maintaining organizational integrity.

- **Adoption of Advanced Technologies**: Utilizing cutting-edge technologies can significantly extend the capabilities and scope of quality goals, promoting more ambitious targets.

Strategies for Implementing Quality Goals

Successful deployment of quality goals involves essential steps:

1. **Comprehensive Communication**: Ensuring that goals are well communicated throughout the organization to secure alignment and commitment.

2. **Adequate Resource Allocation**: Providing necessary resources, including budget, manpower, and technology, to back the pursuit of these goals.

3. **Enhancing Operational Processes**: Regularly upgrading processes to eliminate inefficiencies and support the achievement of quality objectives.

4. **Continuous Monitoring and Adjustment**: Setting up regular tracking mechanisms to monitor progress towards the goals and making necessary adjustments based on empirical data.

For instance, in an industrial setting, applying real-time data analytics might be crucial for monitoring quality control:

```python
# Python pseudocode for applying real-time analytics to monitor product quality

def assess_production_quality(data):
    # Utilize advanced analytics to evaluate quality metrics
    quality_metrics = analyze_data_for_defects(data)
    suggest_improvements_based_on_metrics(quality_metrics)

def analyze_data_for_defects(data):
    # Implement algorithms to identify and analyze quality defects
    pass

def suggest_improvements_based_on_metrics(metrics):
    # Develop strategies to mitigate identified defects
    pass

# Gathering and analyzing data from manufacturing processes
manufacturing_data = fetch_production_data()
assess_production_quality(manufacturing_data)
```

Conclusion

Establishing well-defined quality goals is essential for any enterprise looking to boost its competitive edge and customer satisfaction. By strategically planning and diligently implementing SMART quality goals, organizations can instill a pervasive culture of quality that permeates every aspect of their operations, driving continuous improvement and achieving substantial business success.

Chapter Two

Risk Management Fundamentals

Understanding Risk in Software Projects

Effective risk management is key to the success of software projects, essential for addressing potential barriers that could impact key project metrics such as delivery timelines, budget adherence, and technical specifications. This necessitates not only a reactive approach to resolving issues as they arise but also a proactive strategy for anticipating and mitigating potential disruptions, given the unpredictable nature of software development.

Classification and Origins of Risk in Software Development

Risk in software projects can be understood as any factor or condition that might negatively influence the project's successful completion. These risks stem from various sources:

1. **Technical Risks:** These risks involve complications like persistent software glitches, challenges with systems integration, or the use of outdated technologies that may lead to accumulations of technical debt.

2. **Project Management Risks:** These encompass issues related to the management and logistical aspects of a project such as inefficient resource distribution,

poor timing management, or scope creep beyond initial estimates.

3. **Organizational Risks:** Internal changes such as strategic redirections, staff turnover, or budgetary reductions also represent significant risks.

4. **External Risks:** These risks arise from factors outside the organization, including market instability, regulatory changes, or economic downturns.

Identifying and categorizing these risks is fundamental to developing strategies to effectively mitigate them during the project's lifecycle.

Risk Identification and Assessment Techniques

Identifying potential risks involves gathering insights from all project stakeholders, including project managers, developers, clients, and users. Methods such as brainstorming, expert interviews, the Delphi technique, and the examination of data from comparable past projects are beneficial in this phase.

Following the identification, it's crucial to assess these risks by determining their likelihood of occurrence and the potential severity of their impact. This step is vital for prioritizing the risks, thereby enabling more focused management efforts.

Approaches to Risk Mitigation

Once risks are prioritized, strategies to mitigate these risks need to be formulated. Common mitigation strategies include:

- **Avoidance:** Changing the project's plan to sidestep potential risks entirely.

- **Reduction:** Taking proactive measures to decrease the likelihood or minimize the impact of risks.

- **Transfer:** Shifting the burden of risk to a third party, such as through outsourcing or insurance.

- **Acceptance:** Choosing to accept certain risks when mitigation is impractical, typically applicable to less critical risks.

For example, conducting comprehensive testing or initiating a phased rollout might be strategic for mitigating risks associated with new technology implementations.

Implementing a Risk Management Framework

Effective risk management demands ongoing vigilance and adjustments, necessitating continual reassessments and strategy refinements. Utilizing advanced risk management software can support these efforts by automating the tracking and management of risks. Here's how such a tool might be implemented:

```python
# Python code snippet for risk management automation
def track_project_risks(risks):
    for risk in risks:
        risk_score = risk['probability'] * risk['impact']
        if risk_score > established_threshold:
            alert_project_leaders(risk['description'])

risks = [
    {'description': 'Inadequate developer expertise', 'probability': 0.55,
        'impact': 7},
    {'description': 'Legislative changes impacting compliance', 'probability': 0
        .35, 'impact': 9},
]
established_threshold = 5
track_project_risks(risks)
```

This script helps compute a risk score for each identified risk by multiplying its probability by its impact, triggering alerts for risks that exceed a predefined threshold.

Conclusion

Meticulous risk management is critical for guiding software projects to successful conclusions. By methodically identifying, assessing, and mitigating risks, project teams can substantially enhance their management strategies and operational efficiencies, ensuring that projects meet their scheduled goals, budget, and quality criteria. Implementing a structured risk management protocol allows teams to effectively tackle potential challenges, optimizing the chances of project success.

Risk Identification Techniques

Risk identification is integral to project management, serving to detect potential issues early that could negatively impact a project's key deliverables, such as schedule, budget, and quality. This step is foundational for crafting effective mitigation strategies that help ensure project stability and success. Below we explore various methodologies for identifying risks, detailing how they function and their benefits.

Prominent Methods for Risk Identification

1. **Brainstorming:** This widely-used technique involves assembling all project stakeholders to collaboratively identify potential risks in an uninhibited, supportive environment. The effectiveness of brainstorming largely

depends on creating a setting where participants feel encouraged to share and discuss ideas openly.

2. **Interviews:** Targeted interviews with experienced stakeholders can help unearth risks that may not be immediately apparent. These conversations leverage the historical knowledge and insights of individuals who have encountered similar challenges in past projects.

3. **Delphi Technique:** This method uses anonymous feedback from a panel of experts, who provide their insights in multiple rounds of surveys. Each round refines the group's responses based on collective input, gradually building towards a consensus on the identified risks.

4. **Checklists:** Utilizing checklists based on historical data from related projects prompts teams to consider a spectrum of pre-identified risks, adapting them to the current project's context.

5. **SWOT Analysis:** Adapting SWOT analysis to focus on the Weaknesses and Threats provides a strategic view of potential internal and external risks, making it valuable early in the project planning stage.

6. **Root Cause Analysis:** Methods like the "5 Whys" and "Fishbone Diagram" help trace risks back to their fundamental causes, which is critical for developing strategies that address the root problems rather than just symptoms.

Implementing Risk Identification Techniques

For these methods to be effective, they need to be implemented in a cohesive manner, often integrating outputs from one method into another to deepen understanding and coverage. Advanced project management software can significantly enhance this integration, providing tools for documentation, collaboration, and analysis. Here's how such software might be used to facilitate the Delphi method:

```python
# Python script to aid in the organization of feedback for the Delphi method
def compile_delphi_feedback(feedback_sessions):
    feedback_collection = {}
    for expert_id, feedback in feedback_sessions.items():
        for risk, impact_level in feedback.items():
            if risk in feedback_collection:
                feedback_collection[risk].append(impact_level)
            else:
                feedback_collection[risk] = [impact_level]
    return feedback_collection

# Example data structure for expert feedback rounds
delphi_input = {
    'expert1': {'risk1': 'high impact', 'risk2': 'medium impact'},
    'expert2': {'risk1': 'high impact', 'risk2': 'low impact'},
    'expert3': {'risk1': 'medium impact', 'risk3': 'high impact'},
}

# Aggregating and processing expert feedback
final_feedback = compile_delphi_feedback(delphi_input)
print(final_feedback)
```

This script assists in organizing and analyzing feedback from multiple experts, simplifying the process of building consensus on risk assessments.

Conclusion

Using a diverse set of risk identification techniques is fundamental in proactive risk management within project management. By effectively employing these techniques and supporting them with appropriate digital tools, project managers can anticipate potential issues more reliably, thereby preparing more robustly for project challenges. This strategic approach enhances project resilience, ensures smoother execution, and significantly boosts the likelihood of achieving project objectives.

Risk Assessment and Prioritization

Risk assessment and prioritization are vital in managing risks within a project framework. These processes are essential after risks have been identified, as they assess the potential frequency and severity of these risks. Understanding these factors aids in resource allocation and strategic decision-making to mitigate risks effectively. This examination will cover the techniques and tools used in risk assessment and the principles guiding risk prioritization, demonstrating their importance in achieving project objectives.

The Process of Risk Assessment

Risk assessment investigates the probability and impact of identified risks, providing a basis for understanding which risks could most significantly affect the project. This step is fundamental for prioritizing risks and strategizing their mitigation.

Techniques for Assessing Risks

1. **Qualitative Assessment:** This approach involves subjective evaluation of risks, categorizing them according to their perceived severity and likelihood on a scale from low to high. It is simple and quick, suitable for smaller or less complex projects.

2. **Quantitative Assessment:** This technique quantifies risks by assigning numerical values to their probability and impact, allowing for an objective comparison across all identified risks. It is particularly useful in data-driven environments.

3. **Integrated Methods:** Combining qualitative and quantitative assessments can provide a more comprehensive view, leveraging detailed numerical data where available and expert judgment where it is not.

Tools for Risk Assessment

A variety of tools are employed to facilitate thorough and effective risk assessment:

- **Risk Matrices:** These tools plot risks on a grid defined by likelihood and impact axes, aiding in the visual differentiation of risk severity.

- **Decision Trees:** These graphical representations model possible decisions and their consequences, including costs and outcomes, providing a structured way to anticipate potential risks.

- **Monte Carlo Simulations:** This statistical technique forecasts the probability of various outcomes in processes defined by random variables, useful for modeling the potential variability in risk outcomes.

Criteria for Risk Prioritization

Once risks are assessed, they must be prioritized to focus resources effectively on the most significant threats.

Principles for Prioritizing Risks

- **Impact on Project Deliverables:** Risks with potential to significantly disrupt project deliverables such as scope, budget, or timeline receive higher priority.

- **Stakeholder Significance:** Risks that significantly concern key stakeholders or involve compliance and regulatory requirements are prioritized to ensure stakeholder satisfaction and legal adherence.

- **Resource Availability:** The availability and allocation of resources necessary to mitigate risks also influence their prioritization. Risks requiring more resources may be managed differently based on available capabilities.

Implementing Risk Assessment

Effective implementation of risk assessment involves dynamic and continuous evaluation of risks throughout the project lifecycle. For example, integrating risk assessment within project management software can automate and simplify the process:

```python
import numpy as np

def create_risk_matrix(risks):
    matrix = np.zeros((5, 5))  # Define a simple 5x5 risk matrix
    for risk in risks:
        impact, likelihood = risk['impact'], risk['likelihood']
        matrix[impact-1][likelihood-1] += 1  # Populate matrix based on risk evaluations
    return matrix

# Example risks
risks = [{'impact': 3, 'likelihood': 5, 'description': 'Critical software failure'},
         {'impact': 1, 'likelihood': 2, 'description': 'Minor stakeholder issues'},
         {'impact': 5, 'likelihood': 3, 'description': 'Severe budget overrun'}]

# Create and display the risk matrix
risk_eval_matrix = create_risk_matrix(risks)
print("Risk Evaluation Matrix:\n", risk_eval_matrix)
```

This script helps to visually organize and assess risks based on their likelihood and impact, facilitating strategic responses tailored to the prioritized risks.

Conclusion

Risk assessment and prioritization are essential for managing the uncertainties inherent in project management effectively. By employing detailed assessment techniques and appropriate prioritization principles, project managers can better prepare for and mitigate the impact of risks, thereby safeguarding project success and enhancing project resilience.

Chapter Three

Implementing Risk Management Strategies

Strategies for Risk Mitigation

In project management, effectively mitigating risks is crucial to safeguard the project from potential threats that could compromise its objectives related to schedule, budget, and quality. This entails deploying a set of targeted strategies that help minimize or altogether avoid the impacts of identified risks. This article explores different risk mitigation strategies and discusses how to effectively apply them to enhance project success.

Commonly Used Risk Mitigation Strategies

Selecting the right risk mitigation strategy is dependent on the specific risks involved and their potential to impact the project negatively. The main strategies employed include:

1. **Risk Avoidance:** This strategy involves making adjustments to the project plan to entirely evade the risk. It is generally used when the risk presents a significant threat that could potentially derail the project. This may involve changing methodologies, technologies, or even some project goals.

2. **Risk Reduction:** Also known as risk control, this strategy aims to decrease both the likelihood and the impact of the risk. Methods could include improving operational processes, increasing safety measures, or reallocating resources to more critical tasks.

3. **Risk Transfer:** This approach shifts the risk to another party, often through insurance or by subcontracting elements of the project to external specialists who can manage the risk better.

4. **Risk Acceptance:** This strategy is adopted when the cost of mitigating the risk exceeds the benefit. Here, the risk is acknowledged, and plans are made to handle its potential impacts. This often involves setting aside a contingency budget or resources to deal with the risk should it occur.

Steps for Effective Implementation of Risk Mitigation

Implementing risk mitigation strategies effectively requires careful planning and execution:

- **Developing Mitigation Plans:** Each identified risk should have a specific mitigation plan that outlines detailed steps, resource allocation, and timelines for addressing the risk.

- **Integrating Strategies into the Project Plan:** These strategies need to be seamlessly incorporated into the overall project management plan to ensure that they align with and support the achievement of project objectives.

- **Ongoing Monitoring and Adaptation:** Risk mitigation is an ongoing process that requires continuous monitoring to assess the effectiveness of the strategies being implemented and to make necessary adjustments in response to changes in project dynamics or external factors.

Leveraging Technology in Risk Mitigation

Project management software plays a crucial role in enhancing the efficiency and effectiveness of risk mitigation strategies. Such software can automate the tracking and management of risks and their mitigation processes. Here's an example of how software can be used:

```python
# Python script for automated risk mitigation management
def manage_risk_responses(risks, thresholds):
    for risk in risks:
        combined_score = risk['probability'] * risk['impact']
        if combined_score >= thresholds['high']:
            trigger_mitigation(risk['description'], 'Implement high-impact risk
                mitigation measures.')
        elif combined_score >= thresholds['medium']:
            trigger_mitigation(risk['description'], 'Prepare medium-impact risk
                response plan.')

def trigger_mitigation(risk_description, action):
    # This function could be linked to project management software for
        notifications
    print(f"Action Required: {action} | Risk: {risk_description}")

# Risk data and threshold settings
risks = [
    {'description': 'Legal compliance issues', 'probability': 0.4, 'impact': 9}
    ,
    {'description': 'Technological failures', 'probability': 0.6, 'impact': 7}
]
thresholds = {'high': 25, 'medium': 15}

# Running the risk management script
manage_risk_responses(risks, thresholds)
```

This script evaluates the risks based on their potential impact and triggers corresponding mitigation actions based on predefined thresholds, helping streamline the risk management process.

Conclusion

Risk mitigation is a fundamental aspect of project management that ensures potential threats do not derail the project. By applying strategic mitigation techniques and leveraging advanced project management tools, project managers can effectively minimize risk impacts, ensuring smoother project execution and increasing the likelihood of project success.

Risk Transfer, Avoidance, and Acceptance

In project management, navigating potential threats with strategic risk management techniques such as risk transfer, risk avoidance, and risk acceptance is crucial. These strategies help mitigate the negative impacts of risks, ensuring that projects can proceed smoothly and meet their objectives. This discussion delves into the nuances of these strategies, explaining when and how they are most effectively utilized.

Risk Transfer

Risk transfer involves reallocating the potential consequences of a risk to a third party. It is often achieved through methods like insurance or outsourcing.

1. **Insurance:** One of the most common forms of risk transfer, purchasing insurance allows a project to manage potential financial losses due to unforeseen events by paying a premium.

2. **Outsourcing:** Delegating high-risk tasks to external specialists can reduce the likelihood of failures within critical project components. For example, outsourcing complex IT tasks to a specialized firm can alleviate the risk of technical issues.

While risk transfer can incur costs such as premiums or higher operational expenses, the protection it offers against significant threats often justifies the expenditure.

Risk Avoidance

Risk avoidance aims to completely eliminate exposure to a risk by changing the project's plan or methodology. This approach is decisive but can sometimes lead to increased project costs or missed opportunities.

1. **Modifying Project Scope or Methodology:** Projects might avoid risks by altering their scope or the methods employed. For instance, opting for proven technology over a novel but untested approach can sidestep potential compliance issues.

2. **Investing in Safety Enhancements:** Particularly in industries like construction, avoiding risk might mean investing heavily in safety protocols and equipment to preempt potential accidents.

Risk avoidance can be an effective strategy but may require significant alterations to initial project plans, potentially leading to higher costs or extended timelines.

Risk Acceptance

Risk acceptance involves recognizing and preparing to manage the consequences of a risk without taking steps to prevent the risk itself. It is typically chosen when the costs of mitigation are disproportionate to the potential damage.

1. **Passive Acceptance:** This approach does nothing beyond acknowledging the existence of the risk. It is suitable for risks that are unlikely to occur or will have minimal impact.

2. **Active Acceptance:** This proactive approach involves preparing for the impact of the risk with contingency plans or budget reserves.

Risk acceptance is commonly applied to risks considered to be of lower priority or where resources are insufficient to implement other mitigation strategies.

Practical Application and Integration

Integrating these risk mitigation strategies into project management involves careful planning and ongoing monitoring. Modern project management tools can facilitate the tracking and implementation of these strategies. Here's how a simple software tool might help in managing these strategies:

```python
# Python script for tracking risk management strategies
def execute_risk_strategies(risks):
    for risk in risks:
        if risk['strategy'] == 'transfer':
            print(f"Risk transferred to {risk['partner']}: {risk['description']}"
                )
        elif risk['strategy'] == 'avoid':
            print(f"Risk avoided by changing approach: {risk['description']}")
        elif risk['strategy'] == 'accept':
            print(f"Risk accepted: {risk['description']}")

# Example data for risks
risks = [
    {'description': 'Compliance risks due to new regulations', 'strategy':
        'transfer', 'partner': 'compliance consultant'},
    {'description': 'Potential delays from untested software', 'strategy':
        'avoid'},
    {'description': 'Minor budget fluctuations', 'strategy': 'accept'}
]

# Managing risks with predefined strategies
execute_risk_strategies(risks)
```

This Python script categorizes risks based on the selected mitigation strategy, facilitating the management process within a project management tool.

Conclusion

Employing risk transfer, avoidance, and acceptance strategically within project management is essential for controlling potential disruptions and ensuring project success. By understanding and applying these strategies effectively, project managers can enhance their ability to navigate uncertainties, maintaining control over project outcomes and optimizing resource allocation.

Creating a Risk Management Plan

A risk management plan is integral to ensuring that potential project disruptions are foreseen and mitigated effectively, thereby securing a project's objectives. This document outlines the procedure for building an effective risk management plan, from risk detection to response formulation, and highlights the advantage of utilizing modern technologies to augment these processes.

Purpose of a Risk Management Plan

The risk management plan prepares project teams to handle unexpected challenges proactively. It aims to minimize potential negative impacts and to uphold the project's trajectory towards its goals. Such planning is crucial for maintaining project integrity and efficiency.

Steps for Formulating a Risk Management Plan

1. Identifying Risks

The process begins with a comprehensive identification of potential risks through collaborative sessions involving stakeholders and subject matter experts. This stage catalogs possible issues that could arise from various sources including technical, operational, financial, and regulatory domains.

2. Analyzing Risks

Following identification, each risk undergoes a detailed analysis to evaluate its impact and the likelihood of occurrence. This step helps prioritize the risks by understanding which ones pose the greatest threat and require immediate attention.

3. Prioritizing Risks

Risks are then categorized based on their severity and the probability of their occurrence. This prioritization helps in allocating appropriate resources and formulating focused strategies for the most threatening risks.

4. Developing Mitigation Strategies

Specific strategies are tailored for each risk according to its classification. These can range from avoidance and mitigation to transfer or acceptance, depending on what is most suitable. The plan should clearly outline the measures to be taken, assign responsibility, and allocate resources effectively.

5. Ongoing Monitoring and Adaptation

A risk management plan is not static; it requires continuous monitoring and timely revisions to adapt to new risks or changes in the project's environment. Regular updates ensure that the plan remains relevant and that the strategies are effective.

Technological Integration in Risk Management

The integration of technology significantly streamlines the management of risk. Project management software can automate tracking, updating, and communicating the stages of risk management. Below is an example Python script that demonstrates how technology can facilitate the updating of a risk management plan:

```python
import pandas as pd

# Example setup for a risk management table
risk_details = {
    'Risk': ['Hardware malfunction', 'Exceeding budget', 'Non-compliance with regulations'],
    'Priority': ['High', 'Medium', 'High'],
    'Status': ['Addressing', 'Monitoring', 'Pending']
}

risk_registry = pd.DataFrame(risk_details)

# Function to update the status of risks
def change_risk_status(risk_name, status_update):
    risk_registry.loc[risk_registry['Risk'] == risk_name, 'Status'] = status_update
    print(f"Updated Risk Management Registry:\n{risk_registry}")

# Applying the function to change a risk's status
change_risk_status('Non-compliance with regulations', 'Compliance achieved')
```

This Python script uses the pandas library to manage a risk registry effectively, allowing for quick updates to risk statuses and ensuring that all team members have current information on risk management efforts.

Conclusion

Building and maintaining a robust risk management plan is essential for the successful completion of projects. Through systematic risk management—complemented by strategic planning, regular revisions, and the support of advanced technology—project managers can ensure that projects are well-equipped to navigate uncertainties and achieve their planned objectives.

Chapter Four

Quality Metrics and Analysis

Advanced Metrics for Measuring Software Quality

In contemporary software development, high-quality software is essential for satisfying user demands and retaining a competitive advantage. Advanced metrics are crucial for deeply analyzing software quality, shedding light on its performance, maintainability, and reliability. This article examines several pivotal metrics that are integral to conducting an exhaustive assessment of software quality.

Role of Quality Metrics in Software Development

Quality metrics crucially measure software's operational performance and its adherence to set standards. These metrics are invaluable for early identification of potential problems, allowing for efficient and cost-effective solutions that adhere to project timelines. Additionally, they confirm that the software meets industry standards and satisfies regulatory requirements.

Key Advanced Metrics for Quality Evaluation

1. Cyclomatic Complexity

Developed by Thomas J. McCabe in 1976, cyclomatic complexity quantifies the number of linearly independent paths through a program's source code. It serves as a gauge of the code's complexity, with lower values typically indicating that the code is simpler and thus easier to test, understand, and maintain.

Python Example for Cyclomatic Complexity:

Here is a Python code snippet that demonstrates how to calculate cyclomatic complexity for a basic function:

```python
def example_function(x):
    if x > 10:
        return x + 1
    elif x > 5:
        return x - 1
    else:
        return x

# Function to calculate Cyclomatic Complexity
def calculate_cc(edges, nodes):
    return edges - nodes + 2

# Assuming:
# edges = 3 (paths: >10, >5, else)
# nodes = 4 (if, elif, else, return)
cyclomatic_complexity = calculate_cc(3, 4)
print(f"Cyclomatic Complexity: {cyclomatic_complexity}")
```

2. Maintainability Index

This index evaluates the ease with which software can be maintained, factoring in lines of code, cyclomatic complexity, and Halstead volume. It scores from -infinity to 171, with higher values indicating better maintainability.

3. Code Churn

Code churn measures the volume of code modifications over a designated period, reflecting the software's stability. Elevated churn rates may indicate frequent changes that could potentially undermine the software's stability and quality.

4. Technical Debt

Technical debt quantifies the cost of future corrections due to initial expedient yet suboptimal software development choices. This metric evaluates aspects such as code complexity, duplication, compliance with coding standards, and the presence of potential bugs.

5. Bug Escape Rate

This metric tracks the ratio of bugs found post-release by users against those identified during testing. A lower bug escape rate suggests more effective testing practices and higher overall software quality.

Conclusion

Leveraging advanced metrics to evaluate software quality offers profound insights into a software's development process and its ultimate quality. These metrics significantly guide strategic decisions throughout the software development lifecycle, promoting the delivery of reliable products that meet user expectations. By consistently applying and reviewing these metrics, development teams can substantially improve both the quality of their software and their project management efficiency.

Tools for Tracking and Analyzing Metrics

In the competitive arena of software development, maintaining optimal software quality is vital for customer satisfaction and achieving strategic business objectives. To thoroughly assess software attributes like performance, reliability, and maintainability, advanced tools for monitoring and analyzing metrics are indispensable. This article explores several key tools essential for effective metric measurement and interpretation in software development.

Relevance of Metric Analysis and Tracking Tools

Metric tracking and analysis tools are integral to software development for several reasons:

- **Transparency and Insight**: They provide clear visibility into development processes, allowing teams to measure their performance against objectives.

- **Proactive Issue Resolution**: Early identification of potential problems enables teams to address issues before they escalate, improving project management.

- **Operational Efficiency**: Automation of data collection and analysis saves time, allowing developers to concentrate on critical tasks.

- **Consistent Quality Assurance**: Regular monitoring helps ensure that products meet required quality standards and remain consistent across updates.

Leading Tools for Software Metric Analysis

1. Jira Software

Jira is highly regarded for its project management features, particularly in agile software development settings. It efficiently tracks issues, tasks, and bugs, providing valuable metrics like task completion rates and development velocities.

- **Customizable Reporting**: Jira's customizable dashboards and reports help in managing and visualizing important metrics, facilitating effective project management.

- **Integration Features**: It integrates smoothly with various other platforms, enhancing its functionality for comprehensive metric tracking.

2. Grafana

Grafana is an open-source tool celebrated for its powerful monitoring and visualization capabilities, ideal for interpreting complex datasets from multiple sources.

- **Advanced Visualization Options**: Grafana allows users to create dynamic visualizations, which are crucial for monitoring complex metrics such as network throughput and application health.

- **Integration with Multiple Data Sources**: It supports data integration from various monitoring tools like Prometheus, and logging from sources like Elasticsearch, ensuring a versatile data aggregation capability.

3. Prometheus

Prometheus is designed for monitoring and alerting, particularly effective in managing time-series data.

- **Detailed Monitoring Capabilities**: Its strong suit is handling time-series data, which enables detailed monitoring of metrics over time.
- **Alerting Functionality**: Prometheus can trigger alerts based on specific data conditions, aiding in quick response and issue resolution.

4. New Relic

New Relic offers a set of cloud-based tools for real-time monitoring and analytics across software stacks.

- **Real-Time Data Monitoring**: Its real-time monitoring capabilities provide instant feedback on application and system performance.
- **Comprehensive Analytical Tools**: New Relic includes detailed analysis options for deep dives into transactions and database operations, essential for thorough performance evaluations.

5. SonarQube

SonarQube is known for its continuous code quality checks, using automated reviews to detect and resolve issues in code across over twenty programming languages.

- **Automated Quality Checks**: It continuously analyzes code for bugs, security vulnerabilities, and code smells, ensuring high-quality code development.

- **Quality Gate Standards**: With Quality Gates, SonarQube enforces certain quality standards that codes must meet before production, helping to maintain code integrity and reduce technical debt.

Example of Using Prometheus with Python for Performance Monitoring:

Here's a straightforward demonstration of integrating Prometheus with a Python application to track performance:

```python
from prometheus_client import start_http_server, Summary
import random
import time

# Set up a metric to monitor the time spent processing requests.
REQUEST_TIME = Summary('request_processing_seconds', 'Time spent processing requests')

# Decorate a function to record its performance.
@REQUEST_TIME.time()
def process_request(t):
    """A mock function to simulate request processing time."""
    time.sleep(t)

if __name__ == '__main__':
    # Start the server to expose metrics.
    start_http_server(8000)
    # Simulate processing requests indefinitely.
    while True:
        process_request(random.random())
```

This script illustrates how Prometheus's Python client can be used to monitor how long it takes to process requests, exposing these metrics on a local web server.

Conclusion

Choosing appropriate tools for tracking and analyzing metrics is crucial for teams aiming to enhance their software development practices. By deploying these advanced tools, teams can ensure that they not only maintain but improve their product quality, streamline their development processes, and better manage their projects.

Using Metrics to Guide QA Decisions

In the software development industry, the systematic incorporation of metrics within Quality Assurance (QA) practices is essential for ensuring optimal product performance, fulfilling user expectations, and enhancing process efficiency. Metrics provide QA teams with concrete data that underpin their decisions, pinpoint improvement needs, evaluate the efficacy of testing methods, and refine the development process. This article explores how specific metrics fundamentally influence QA decision-making, thereby enriching the QA process and ensuring software products meet both functional and user requirements.

Importance of Metrics in QA

Metrics are vital tools in QA, offering quantifiable insights that allow teams to make informed, accurate decisions. They help in assessing the impact of QA strategies, identifying vulnerabilities in the software, and efficiently managing resources.

Essential Metrics for Influencing QA Decisions

1. Code Coverage

Code coverage measures the extent of source code that has been executed during tests, providing an indicator of testing completeness. It aids QA teams in identifying untested segments of code. High levels of code coverage typically indicate comprehensive testing coverage, although it is crucial to ensure the quality of tests remains high.

Illustrative Example with a Code Coverage Tool: Consider using a code coverage tool like Istanbul to assess a JavaScript function:

```javascript
// Example demonstrating Istanbul's capability to assess code coverage for a function
function multiply(a, b) {
    return a * b;
}

// Test case for the multiply function
describe('multiply function', function() {
    it('multiplies two numbers', function() {
        expect(multiply(4, 3)).toBe(12);
    });
});
```

Executing this test with Istanbul will generate a coverage report, informing subsequent testing strategies.

2. Defect Density

Defect density calculates the total number of defects found per unit size of the software, often per thousand lines of code. This metric highlights critical areas within the application that may require more focused testing or improvements.

3. Test Case Effectiveness

This metric evaluates the proportion of test cases that successfully detect defects, indicating the quality and appropriateness of the test cases used. Effective test cases suggest a robust testing framework.

4. Mean Time to Detect (MTTD)

MTTD measures the average duration taken to identify defects, offering insights into the responsiveness of the testing process. Faster detection times typically reflect more effective testing tools and methodologies.

5. Mean Time to Repair (MTTR)

MTTR quantifies the average time required to fix a defect. It is an essential metric for assessing the agility and efficiency of the QA team. A shorter MTTR often signifies a more capable and responsive QA process.

Leveraging QA Metrics Strategically

Continuous Refinement Through Monitoring

Ongoing monitoring of these metrics enables QA teams to continually adjust and improve their testing strategies. Persistent issues in certain areas, as indicated by high defect density, might suggest the need for additional testing or code changes.

Resource Optimization

Metrics such as defect density and test case effectiveness facilitate informed decisions on resource allocation, ensuring that QA efforts are both effective and efficient.

Predictive Analysis

Utilizing historical metrics data, QA teams can employ predictive analytics to forecast potential future issues, allowing for preemptive action and better resource planning.

```python
# Example of using linear regression for predictive analytics in Python
from sklearn.linear_model import LinearRegression
import numpy as np

# Sample data: Weekly defect counts
weeks = np.array([1, 2, 3, 4, 5, 6]).reshape(-1, 1)
defects = np.array([4, 10, 15, 20, 18, 22])

# Fit a linear regression model
model = LinearRegression()
model.fit(weeks, defects)

# Predict defects for an upcoming week
future_week = np.array([[7]])
predicted_defects = model.predict(future_week)
print(f"Predicted defects for week 7: {predicted_defects[0]}")
```

Conclusion

Metrics are indispensable in QA for software development, providing essential data that support making strategic, data-driven decisions. By effectively employing these metrics, companies can significantly boost their QA activities, leading to software that not only adheres to technical standards but also exceeds user expectations.

Chapter Five

Cost Management in QA

Analyzing the Costs of Quality

In the field of software development, proficiently managing and understanding the expenses linked to maintaining high-quality standards are critical for project viability and success. These expenses, termed the "costs of quality" (CoQ), are bifurcated into costs that contribute to achieving quality (conformance costs) and those incurred due to quality shortcomings (non-conformance costs). Effective oversight and scrutiny of these costs are pivotal for firms aiming to refine their operational effectiveness and remain financially prudent while ensuring product excellence. This article delineates the various facets of CoQ, articulates methodologies for their scrutiny, and considers their ramifications on software project management.

Breakdown of Costs of Quality

The framework of CoQ was introduced by Joseph Juran, and it encompasses all expenses incurred throughout the product lifecycle that relate to both attaining and failing to achieve established quality benchmarks.

1. Prevention Costs

These expenditures are aimed at defect prevention before they manifest. This category includes spending on activities like requirements analysis, design and code reviews, test strategy formulation, and training initiatives to augment developer competencies.

2. Appraisal Costs

These are costs associated with evaluating products to ensure they meet quality standards and performance specifications. This group includes expenses for conducting testing, periodic evaluations during the development lifecycle, audits, and acquiring or developing quality assurance software tools.

3. Internal Failure Costs

Incurred when defects are detected before the product reaches the customer, these costs involve the financial outlays for remediation, corrective actions, and the operational downtimes required to address the defects. Additional expenses in this category are for debugging, re-testing, and the delays in product launches due to these activities.

4. External Failure Costs

These costs arise when defects are recognized only after the product has been delivered to customers. They can encompass warranty claims, product recalls, customer service expenses related to these defects, and potentially more severe financial repercussions such as reputation damage or legal consequences. Generally, external failure costs are higher than internal failure costs due to the broader impact and the complexity involved in rectifying issues that have affected end-users.

Methods for Analyzing Costs of Quality

For organizations to effectively minimize and manage CoQ, a comprehensive analysis of these costs based on detailed data for each type is imperative. Such scrutiny typically employs various analytical techniques.

Analytical Approaches for CoQ:

- **Activity-Based Costing (ABC):** This method attributes costs to particular activities or processes within quality assurance, providing an accurate depiction of where financial resources are being used.

- **Root Cause Analysis (RCA):** This technique aims to pinpoint the underlying reasons for defects, thereby aiding in the targeted application of preventative measures.

- **Statistical Process Control (SPC):** SPC utilizes statistical techniques to monitor and control the manufacturing process, identifying trends that could lead to future quality issues before they escalate into significant problems.

Example: SQL Query for Analyzing Internal Failure Costs

Here is a simple SQL query that might be utilized to examine and understand internal failure costs by assessing the frequency of bug fixes and the average cost associated with each fix:

```sql
-- SQL Query to analyze internal failure costs
SELECT module, COUNT(bug_id) AS total_bugs, AVG(cost) AS average_cost_per_bug
FROM Bugs
WHERE status = 'fixed'
GROUP BY module
ORDER BY total_bugs DESC;
```

This query helps to identify which modules are consuming the most resources in terms of debugging and fixing, allowing for strategic decisions regarding process improvements or resource reallocation.

Impact of CoQ on Software Project Management

Managing CoQ effectively influences several aspects of project management:

- **Budgeting Accuracy:** Comprehensive CoQ analysis facilitates more precise budget forecasts by incorporating anticipated quality-related expenses.

- **Optimized Resource Allocation:** Insights from CoQ analysis enable more strategic resource distribution, prioritizing areas with substantial quality-related costs.

- **Enhanced Risk Management:** Data from CoQ analyses assist in pinpointing high-risk areas, allowing project managers to deploy focused risk mitigation strategies.

Conclusion

CoQ plays a vital role in software development, impacting both the budgetary framework and the operational strategies of projects. By rigorously analyzing these costs, organizations can make strategic decisions that not only curb expenses but also amplify the quality of the software products they deliver. Striking a balance between the costs of preventing defects and those arising from failures is key to financial efficiency and high-quality output.

Budgeting for QA Activities

Effective allocation of resources for Quality Assurance (QA) in software projects is crucial for delivering products that meet quality standards while controlling costs. Proper budget planning for QA ensures teams have the necessary resources to conduct detailed testing, critical for minimizing defects and associated project risks. This article discusses essential considerations for formulating a QA budget, factors that influence financial decisions in QA, and methods for efficiently managing QA resources.

The Necessity of QA Budgeting

Appropriate budgeting for QA is vital as it directly affects the quality and scope of testing activities. Insufficient budgeting can lead to inadequate testing, potentially resulting in undetected defects, increased post-launch costs, and damage to the product's reputation. On the other hand, a well-allocated QA budget ensures that adequate resources are available for thorough testing, promoting early detection and resolution of issues.

Factors Impacting QA Budgeting

1. Project Scope and Complexity

The scale and complexity of a project are major determinants of the QA budget. Larger and more complex projects require extensive testing efforts, demanding more resources, sophisticated tools, and larger teams. Accurately defining the project scope helps in estimating the required resources for effective QA.

2. Development Methodology

The software development methodology employed, such as Agile or Waterfall, influences how QA activities are integrated and financed. Agile methodologies typically necessitate a more dynamic and comprehensive QA budget due to their iterative nature and continuous integration demands, compared to the more structured Waterfall approach.

3. Historical Data and Performance Metrics

Leveraging data from previous projects can provide insights into prior expenditures and resource utilization, aiding in refining future QA budget forecasts. Utilizing metrics like defect density and mean time to detect (MTTD) assists in tailoring resource allocation based on past performance and identified risks.

4. Risk Assessment

Identifying potential risks related to the software project, whether they are operational, financial, or reputational, is essential for creating an appropriate QA budget. Projects with higher risk profiles may require more rigorous testing and, consequently, a larger budget to mitigate those risks effectively.

Strategic Approaches to QA Budgeting

1. Resource Allocation

Resource allocation should not only address current project needs but also align with broader QA objectives. This involves investing in skilled personnel, up-to-date testing technologies, and ongoing professional development.

2. Flexible Budgeting Framework

Adopting a flexible budgeting approach, especially in Agile settings, allows for modifications in response to evolving project demands and unforeseen challenges.

3. Cost-Benefit Analysis

Executing cost-benefit analyses for different QA initiatives helps prioritize spending on measures that provide the greatest return on investment, focusing on activities that significantly lower defect rates and enhance product stability.

4. Budget Integration

Integrating the QA budget with the overall project budget ensures cohesive collaboration between QA and development teams, optimizing efforts and reducing the likelihood of expensive delays.

Example: Python Tool for Budget Tracking

Here is an example of how a simple Python tool can be used to manage and monitor QA budgeting effectively:

```python
import pandas as pd

# Initialize data for QA budgeting
data = {
    'Activity': ['Unit Testing', 'Automation Setup', 'Performance Testing',
        'Compliance Checks'],
    'Budget': [60000, 40000, 30000, 15000]
}

budget_df = pd.DataFrame(data)

# Function to adjust budget for specific activities
def adjust_budget(activity, new_amount):
    global budget_df
    if activity in budget_df['Activity'].values:
        budget_df.loc[budget_df['Activity'] == activity, 'Budget'] = new_amount
        print("Revised Budget:\n", budget_df)
    else:
        print("Activity not listed.")

# Example of budget adjustment
adjust_budget('Compliance Checks', 18000)
```

This Python script uses pandas to manage a budget data frame for QA activities, enabling easy adjustments and ensuring accurate tracking of budget allocations.

Conclusion

Strategic budgeting for QA is integral to the success of software development projects, ensuring they not only achieve desired quality levels but also stay within financial limits. By understanding key budgeting factors and applying effective resource management strategies, organizations can maximize their QA efforts and deliver high-quality software products efficiently.

Cost-Benefit Analysis in QA Projects

Effective management of Quality Assurance (QA) is vital in software development for ensuring that products meet established quality criteria and stay within allocated budgets. QA is crucial for early detection of defects and confirming that products conform to their specifications. Despite its importance, QA incurs significant costs. A cost-benefit analysis (CBA) is crucial for assessing whether the investment in QA delivers sufficient returns, supporting strategic resource allocation decisions.

Exploring Cost-Benefit Analysis for QA

The cost-benefit analysis in QA projects involves evaluating the financial expenditures on QA activities against the derived benefits, such as improved product reliability, reductions in subsequent maintenance costs, and higher levels of customer satisfaction. The primary goal is to ascertain if the benefits outweigh the costs, validating the investments made in QA efforts.

Fundamental Elements of Cost-Benefit Analysis

1. Costs Categorization

In QA, costs can be divided into:

- **Direct costs**: These are explicit expenses associated with the execution of QA activities, which include costs for QA staff, testing infrastructure, and software tools.

- **Indirect costs**: These are costs affected by QA activities but not billed directly to QA. This category includes potential revenue losses from delayed product launches or the impact on brand reputation due to poor quality.

2. Benefits Evaluation

Evaluating the benefits of QA involves considering:

- **Customer satisfaction**: Enhanced product quality often results in greater customer satisfaction, potentially leading to increased loyalty and sales.

- **Decrease in defects**: This lowers the need for customer service and the likelihood of issuing refunds or replacements.

- **Reputation enhancement**: High product quality can improve a company's standing in the market, attracting new customers and expanding business opportunities.

3. Financial Data Analysis

After the costs and benefits are identified and quantified, analyzing these figures to calculate financial metrics such as ROI or NPV helps in determining the economic value of QA investments.

Conducting a Cost-Benefit Analysis in QA

Step 1: Scope Definition

Identify and define the range of QA activities that will be included in the analysis. This might involve specific testing procedures or the overall approach to QA.

Step 2: Estimating Costs

Compile data on all expenses associated with the designated QA activities, taking into account both direct and indirect costs.

Step 3: Projecting Benefits

Estimate the financial benefits expected from the QA activities, considering both immediate savings and long-term gains.

Step 4: Net Benefits Calculation

Determine the net benefits by subtracting the total estimated costs from the estimated benefits. Positive results indicate that the QA activities are economically justified.

Step 5: Sensitivity Analysis

Perform sensitivity analysis to determine how changes in assumptions impact the calculated outcomes. This analysis helps in understanding the robustness of the QA investments against fluctuations in underlying assumptions.

Example: Using Python for Cost-Benefit Calculations

Here's a Python script that exemplifies how to calculate ROI for QA investments:

```python
def calculate_roi(costs, benefits):
    """Function to determine the Return on Investment (ROI) from specified costs
        and benefits."""
    return ((benefits - costs) / costs) * 100

# Example input data
annual_costs = 25000    # Annual costs for QA activities
annual_benefits = 50000 # Estimated annual benefits from improved quality and
    reduced maintenance

# Calculate ROI
roi = calculate_roi(annual_costs, annual_benefits)
print(f"ROI for QA investments is: {roi}%")
```

This script provides a basic method for calculating ROI, giving a clear indicator of the economic effectiveness of QA activities.

Conclusion

Cost-benefit analysis is an essential practice in QA project management, enabling organizations to evaluate whether their expenditures on quality assurance are justifiable from an economic perspective and aligned with strategic goals. By meticulously assessing costs and benefits, organizations can make informed decisions that enhance product quality and optimize financial outcomes, ensuring that QA initiatives contribute positively to overall business objectives.

Chapter Six

Resource Allocation and Optimization

Effective Resource Planning for QA Teams

Resource planning is essential for managing Quality Assurance (QA) operations within software development, ensuring teams efficiently utilize their capabilities to uphold product quality. This process involves the strategic allocation of time, personnel, tools, and budget, aligning QA activities with broader project goals and schedules. This article outlines fundamental practices and methodologies for efficient resource planning, aiming to equip QA teams to handle project challenges effectively and deliver superior software products.

Importance of Resource Planning in QA

Resource planning transcends simple task allocation; it requires a holistic approach that optimizes the use of all available resources to meet detailed testing phases effectively. Proper resource planning helps in reducing wastage and ensures QA teams can achieve their objectives efficiently, without overstretching resources or experiencing significant downtime.

Critical Elements of Resource Planning for QA Teams

1. Comprehensive Understanding of Project Requirements

Accurate resource planning starts with a deep understanding of the project's demands. QA managers must be familiar with the scope, complexity, and specific quality criteria of the project to anticipate the necessary resources adequately. This foresight helps in determining the number of personnel needed, the types of tools required, and the timing for each testing segment.

2. Evaluation of Skills and Resources

Effective allocation hinges on a thorough assessment of the team's skills and the resources at their disposal. Matching team members' skills and experience with appropriate tasks ensures that resources are utilized optimally, promoting productivity and job satisfaction among team members.

3. Strategic Timing and Scheduling

Proper timing and scheduling are pivotal for integrating QA activities seamlessly with the rest of the development workflow. Synchronizing QA tasks with the development stages ensures that testing is both timely and effective, minimizing bottlenecks and idle times.

4. Rigorous Budget Control

Managing the budget is a significant factor in resource planning, as financial constraints often dictate the extent of resource allocation. Effective budget management ensures that QA teams are well-equipped without exceeding financial limits. Adjustments to the budget may be necessary as project requirements evolve or unexpected needs arise.

Strategies for Streamlining Resource Planning

1. Adoption of Resource Management Tools

Modern project management and resource allocation tools can significantly enhance the planning process. These tools facilitate skill matching, provide real-time resource availability updates, and allow for integration with other project management platforms, enabling more dynamic and informed planning.

Example: Simple Resource Management Tool Implementation

Below is a basic example of a resource management tool implemented in Python:

```python
import pandas as pd

# Setting up a sample data frame for QA resources
data = {
    'Name': ['John Doe', 'Jane Smith', 'Alice Johnson'],
    'Skill': ['Automated Testing', 'Security Testing', 'Performance Testing'],
    'Availability': ['Full-time', 'Part-time', 'Full-time']
}

resource_df = pd.DataFrame(data)

# Function to locate QA resources based on specific skills
def locate_resources(skill):
    filtered_resources = resource_df[resource_df['Skill'] == skill]
    print(f"Available Resources for {skill}:\n{filtered_resources}")

# Demonstrating the function
locate_resources('Automated Testing')
```

This Python code creates a database of resources and allows managers to search for QA personnel based on their skills.

2. Ongoing Resource Adjustment

Continual reassessment of resource allocations is crucial, especially in agile project environments where requirements may change rapidly. Regularly updating resource plans ensures that the QA team remains adaptable and responsive to project needs.

3. Encouraging Skill Diversification

Encouraging ongoing training and cross-disciplinary learning within QA teams can broaden their skill sets, reducing dependencies on specific personnel and allowing for more flexible task assignments.

Conclusion

Efficient resource planning is critical for QA teams to effectively perform their roles within software development projects. By thoroughly understanding project requirements, evaluating team capabilities, and utilizing advanced planning tools, QA managers can optimize their resource use. Flexible and dynamic resource management further supports QA teams in maintaining high productivity and meeting project quality goals effectively.

Tools and Techniques for Resource Optimization

Resource optimization is vital across industries such as software development and manufacturing, where operational efficiency and cost management are paramount. This strategic management of resources involves employing the best tools and methodologies to maximize productivity and optimize investment returns. This article discusses various advanced tools and approaches for resource optimization, detailing their functionality and the advantages they offer.

Significance of Resource Optimization

Resource optimization is the strategic deployment and management of company resources to maximize operational effectiveness and improve output quality. It involves meticulous planning and execution to reduce waste, efficiently manage costs, and enhance overall performance by utilizing specific tools and methods for resource management.

Top Tools for Resource Optimization

1. Project Management Tools

Software solutions like Microsoft Project, Asana, and Jira are indispensable for effective resource optimization. These platforms facilitate task scheduling, resource allocation, and progress tracking, essential for managing project timelines and labor effectively. They provide analytics that allows managers to monitor resource usage and productivity, facilitating proactive adjustments.

Example: Managing Tasks with Jira

Jira enables managers to assign tasks effectively according to the team members' skills and availability, ensuring equitable workload distribution and optimal resource use.

```python
# Python script to extract and display tasks from Jira
from jira import JIRA

# Establishing a connection to Jira
jira = JIRA(basic_auth=('your_username', 'your_password'), server='https://your
    -jira-instance')

# Retrieving and displaying open tasks assigned to the user
tasks = jira.search_issues('assignee = currentUser() AND status = "Open"')
for task in tasks:
    print(f"Task {task.key}: {task.fields.summary}")
```

2. Enterprise Resource Planning (ERP) Software

ERP systems such as SAP and Oracle unify various business operations into a single platform, facilitating comprehensive resource planning and management. These systems enhance decision-making capabilities by providing an integrated view of resource allocation across departments.

3. Specialized Optimization Tools

Tools like IBM ILOG CPLEX and Google OR-Tools utilize advanced algorithms and mathematical models to address complex resource allocation challenges, ideal for scenarios requiring dynamic resource scheduling.

Example: Optimizing Routes Using Google OR-Tools

Google OR-Tools efficiently handles logistical challenges like route optimization, minimizing travel time and operational costs.

```python
from ortools.constraint_solver import routing_enums_pb2
from ortools.constraint_solver import pywrapcp

def create_data_model():
    """Setup data for the problem."""
    data = {}
    data['distance_matrix'] = [[0, 6, 9], [6, 0, 5], [9, 5, 0]]  # Distances
        between locations
    data['num_vehicles'] = 1
    data['depot'] = 0
    return data

def main():
    """Solve the routing problem."""
    data = create_data_model()

    # Initialize the routing index manager and routing model.
    manager = pywrapcp.RoutingIndexManager(len(data['distance_matrix']),
        data['num_vehicles'], data['depot'])
    routing = pywrapcp.RoutingModel(manager)

    # Create and register a transit callback.
    transit_callback_index = routing.RegisterTransitCallback(lambda from_index,
        to_index: data['distance_matrix'][manager.IndexToNode(from_index)
        )][manager.IndexToNode(to_index)])
    routing.SetArcCostEvaluatorOfAllVehicles(transit_callback_index)
```

```python
    # Solve the route.
    solution = routing.Solve()
    if solution:
        print('Total distance: {} miles'.format(solution.ObjectiveValue()))
        index = routing.Start(0)
        route = []
        while not routing.IsEnd(index):
            route.append(manager.IndexToNode(index))
            index = solution.Value(routing.Next(index))
        route.append(manager.IndexToNode(index))
        print("Route:", route)
if __name__ == '__main__':
    main()
```

Resource Optimization Techniques

1. Lean Methodology

Applying Lean principles helps significantly reduce waste and increase efficiency through continuous improvement and just-in-time resource use.

2. Six Sigma Techniques

Six Sigma aims to reduce process variability and defects, using statistical methods to streamline processes and improve resource efficiency.

3. Dynamic Capacity Planning

This method adjusts resource levels to accommodate fluctuating demands, ensuring operational effectiveness without resource wastage. Effective capacity planning relies on accurate demand forecasting and adaptable resource management strategies.

Conclusion

Resource optimization is essential for sustaining competitive advantage and achieving excellence in operations. By using advanced tools and adopting proven methodologies, organizations can ensure that resources are effectively utilized, leading to cost reductions and enhanced quality of outputs. These strategies are crucial for driving continuous business improvement and sustainable growth.

Balancing Efficiency and Effectiveness

Navigating the delicate balance between efficiency and effectiveness is crucial for businesses focused on sustainable operational success. Efficiency measures how little resources can be expended to achieve a given output, focusing on cost reduction and process speed. Effectiveness, in contrast, assesses whether the results meet intended goals and quality benchmarks, emphasizing outcome over output.

Distinctions and Dynamics

Efficiency evaluates how economically a business operates, striving to do more with less by minimizing resource expenditure for the maximum output possible. **Effectiveness** deals with meeting target outcomes and ensuring that the results align with strategic goals, measuring the quality and impact of those results.

For instance, a business might operate with high efficiency by producing outputs at a minimal cost, but if these outputs fail to satisfy customer expectations, the business is not effective. Alternatively, a business might achieve all its performance goals (demonstrating effectiveness) but at an unsustainable cost, showing poor efficiency.

Strategies for Harmonizing Efficiency and Effectiveness

1. Adopting Lean Operations

Lean operations help improve both efficiency and effectiveness by removing non-essential operations and focusing on what adds value. By employing methods like continuous improvement (Kaizen), just-in-time inventory (JIT), and value stream mapping, businesses can minimize waste and enhance product quality simultaneously.

2. Technological Integration

Incorporating cutting-edge technology can streamline operations to enhance efficiency and ensure consistent quality, thus affecting effectiveness. Automation, for instance, reduces labor costs and increases production speed while maintaining or improving product quality.

Example of Efficient Automation:

```python
# Python script for automating routine data management tasks
import pandas as pd

# Example data setup
data = {'Name': ['Louis Armstrong', 'Billie Holiday'],
        'Email': ['louis@jazz.com', 'billie@blues.com'],
        'RegistrationDate': ['2023-02-01', '2023-02-02']}

df = pd.DataFrame(data)

def automate_data_management(data_frame):
    for index, row in data_frame.iterrows():
        print(f"Updating record for {row['Name']}: Email - {row['Email']}, Date - {row['RegistrationDate']}")
        # Placeholder for data update logic to a database

automate_data_management(df)
```

This Python example shows how automating data management tasks can save time and reduce errors, enhancing both efficiency and the reliability of data.

3. Strategic Resource Management

Effective resource management ensures optimal use of assets, balancing the right amount of resources for the tasks without overspending, thus maintaining efficiency while achieving desired outcomes.

4. Customer-Oriented Adjustments

Aligning operational adjustments based on customer feedback ensures the effectiveness of the output. Though it may decrease efficiency temporarily, adapting to customer needs enhances product relevance and customer satisfaction.

5. Dual Metrics Approach

Using a dual metrics system that evaluates both efficiency (like time and cost metrics) and effectiveness (customer satisfaction and quality metrics) provides a comprehensive view of organizational performance, guiding balanced operational decisions.

Overcoming Balancing Challenges

Balancing efficiency and effectiveness involves understanding their interdependencies and potential trade-offs. Investments in technologies intended to enhance efficiency might not yield immediate returns, and a strong focus on quality and customer satisfaction can lead to increased costs.

Conclusion

For businesses aiming to thrive, mastering the balance between efficiency and effectiveness is vital. Through strategic resource planning, leveraging technology, implementing lean principles, and maintaining a customer-focused approach, organizations can optimize operations to achieve both operational speed and quality outcomes, ensuring long-term sustainability and competitive advantage.

Chapter Seven

Advanced Test Design Techniques

Designing Tests for Maximum Impact

In the field of software development, the importance of effective testing cannot be overstated. Properly designed testing protocols are key to detecting issues before the product reaches the market, ensuring functionality is as intended, and maximizing user satisfaction. A well-thought-out testing strategy ensures comprehensive coverage that can substantially elevate the product's quality.

Emphasizing the Importance of High-Impact Testing

High-impact testing not only identifies flaws but also verifies the software's robustness, compliance with user expectations, and overall usability. This level of testing prevents costly post-launch repairs and maintains the company's reputation by ensuring a reliable product is delivered.

Effective Testing Strategy Development

1. Set Clear Testing Objectives

The first step in impactful testing involves defining clear and measurable objectives that align with both the business's goals and user expectations. These objectives need to address critical software aspects like functionality, performance, security, and usability.

2. Develop Tests Based on Real-User Scenarios

To ensure software performs optimally in real-world conditions, testing should be based on actual user behavior. This approach allows testers to uncover potential issues that might not manifest in theoretical or controlled environments, thus better prioritizing testing resources.

Example of Realistic User Scenario Testing:

```python
# Python pseudocode for testing an end-to-end shopping scenario on an e-commerce site

def test_full_shopping_experience():
    # User login simulation
    user_login(email="demo@user.com", password="testpass")
    assert is_logged_in(), "User should be logged in successfully"

    # Adding a product to the shopping cart
    product_code = "123ABC"
    add_to_cart(product_code)
    assert check_cart(product_code), "Product should be in the shopping cart"

    # Checking out process simulation
    initiate_checkout()
    submit_payment(method="credit card", amount="120.00")
    assert payment_is_successful(), "Payment should be completed successfully"

    # Logging out
    user_logout()
    assert not is_logged_in(), "User should be logged out"
```

This script ensures each phase of the shopping process works as intended, from logging in to making a purchase and logging out.

3. Test Case Prioritization

It's crucial to prioritize test cases based on their importance and the severity of potential impact. Areas involving significant risk, like security or fundamental functionalities, warrant more intensive testing.

4. Implement Automation for Tests

Automating routine or straightforward tests can enhance efficiency and ensure consistency. Automation proves especially beneficial for regression testing, helping to ensure that new changes do not adversely affect existing functionalities.

5. Iterate Based on Feedback

Testing should be an iterative process that incorporates ongoing feedback from developers, testers, and end-users. This approach ensures testing remains relevant and aligned with the project's needs as they evolve.

Employing Advanced Testing Tools

Leveraging sophisticated testing tools can make the testing process more efficient and effective. Automation tools like Selenium for web interfaces, JUnit for applications written in Java, and PyTest for Python are invaluable for managing and automating testing tasks.

Conclusion

Maximizing the impact of testing in software development requires diligent planning and execution. By clearly defining testing goals, basing tests on realistic user scenarios, prioritizing crucial test areas, automating tests appropriately, and adapting to feedback, development teams can greatly enhance both the efficacy and efficiency of their testing efforts. This comprehensive approach not only helps in thorough defect detection but also significantly boosts the overall quality, reliability, and market readiness of the software, facilitating sustained success and competitive market performance.

Orthogonal Array Testing

Orthogonal Array Testing (OAT) is a sophisticated approach in the software testing domain that uses statistical methods to streamline the testing process by reducing the number of tests needed while ensuring comprehensive coverage. This technique is especially useful when complete factorial testing is impractical due to limitations in time or resources.

Introduction to Orthogonal Array Testing

Orthogonal Array Testing harnesses mathematical principles to efficiently select a subset of test scenarios that optimally cover all possible combinations of inputs and configurations. The foundation of OAT lies in the statistical principle of orthogonality, which ensures that variables are varied systematically to assess their individual and combined impacts on system performance. This method is ideal for testing applications required to operate under a wide array of conditions and configurations, effectively identifying issues related to specific variable interactions.

Advantages of Orthogonal Array Testing

1. **Increased Testing Efficiency**: OAT minimizes the number of necessary test cases, significantly reducing testing time and associated costs.

2. **Ensured Comprehensive Coverage**: It guarantees that all potential interactions of variables are considered by testing each combination at least once, offering thorough coverage with fewer tests.

3. **Systematic Testing Framework**: OAT's structured approach helps in uniformly distributing test cases, minimizing bias and ensuring a balanced representation of all variable interactions.

4. **Facilitated Problem Identification**: The methodical isolation of variable effects simplifies the process of pinpointing defects, enhancing the debugging process.

Implementing Orthogonal Array Testing

Effective implementation of OAT involves several crucial steps:

1. **Define Variables and Their Levels**: Identify the key factors influencing system behavior and the different settings each can take.

2. **Choose a Suitable Orthogonal Array**: Pick an orthogonal array that fits the number of variables and their respective levels, tailored to meet specific interaction coverage needs.

3. **Organize Test Cases According to the Array**: Use the orthogonal array as a guide to systematically assign variable levels across test cases.

4. **Execute Tests and Analyze Results**: Carry out the designated tests as per the orthogonal array setup and

meticulously analyze the data to identify any discrepancies.

Python Implementation Example for Orthogonal Array Testing:

Here's how you can set up an orthogonal array in Python for a system with three variables, demonstrating a practical application:

```python
import numpy as np
# Define the factors with their respective levels
factors = {"Operating System": ["Windows", "macOS"],
           "Browser": ["Firefox", "Chrome"],
           "User Type": ["Administrator", "Standard"]}

# Using an L4 orthogonal array for three factors, each with two levels
oa_l4 = np.array([[0, 0, 0],
                  [0, 1, 1],
                  [1, 0, 1],
                  [1, 1, 0]])

# Mapping orthogonal array to specific test scenarios
def configure_tests(oa, factors):
    test_configurations = []
    factor_list = list(factors.keys())
    for setup in oa:
        configuration = {factor_list[i]: factors[factor_list[i]][level] for i,
            level in enumerate(setup)}
        test_configurations.append(configuration)
    return test_configurations
# Generate and display test configurations
configured_tests = configure_tests(oa_l4, factors)
for idx, config in enumerate(configured_tests, 1):
    print(f"Configuration {idx}: {config}")
```

Conclusion

Orthogonal Array Testing revolutionizes the approach to software testing by leveraging statistical designs to enhance test effectiveness and efficiency. By reducing the volume of test cases while covering extensive variable interactions, OAT not only conserves resources but also maintains a high standard of product quality, proving itself as an indispensable tool in the arsenal of modern software testing methodologies.

Using Design Patterns in Test Creation

Design patterns are essential tools in software engineering, known for solving common structural and behavioral issues. When these patterns are applied to the development of test suites, they enhance the design and execution of tests, making them more efficient, manageable, and scalable.

Relevance of Design Patterns in Testing

Design patterns provide time-tested solutions that streamline the development process, including the creation of sophisticated test frameworks. In the realm of testing, these patterns address challenges like cumbersome test maintenance, test data management, and the scalability of test operations. Utilizing design patterns in testing helps ensure that test suites are robust and can evolve with the application they support.

Benefits of Employing Design Patterns in Testing

1. **Maintenance Efficiency**: Design patterns standardize test creation, making suites easier to update and maintain as application features evolve.

2. **Test Reusability**: Leveraging design patterns makes it easier to replicate and adapt tests for various scenarios, increasing the reusability of test code.

3. **Operational Streamlining**: These patterns can organize and optimize the testing process, reducing the time required to develop and execute tests.

4. **Enhanced Clarity**: Tests crafted using design patterns are more orderly and understandable, which simplifies the process for developers and testers to follow and modify them.

Key Design Patterns Utilized in Test Creation

1. Page Object Pattern: Often used in automated UI testing, this pattern creates a dedicated object for each page within the application, containing all necessary functionalities. This isolates UI changes to object files, minimizing impacts on the test scripts.

Example of Page Object Pattern:

```python
class SettingsPage:
    def __init__(self, driver):
        self.driver = driver
        self.settings_menu = 'settings_menu_id'

    def navigate_to_settings(self):
        self.driver.find_element_by_id(self.settings_menu).click()

# Usage
from selenium import webdriver
driver = webdriver.Chrome()
settings_page = SettingsPage(driver)
settings_page.navigate_to_settings()
```

This approach simplifies the maintenance of test scripts when UI changes occur.

2. Factory Pattern: This pattern is ideal for scenarios where different instances of objects are required for tests. It centralizes object creation, enhancing flexibility in how objects are instantiated.

Example of Factory Pattern:

```python
class NotificationFactory:
    @staticmethod
    def create_notification(notification_type):
        if notification_type == "email":
            return EmailNotification()
        else:
            return SMSNotification()

class EmailNotification:
    def send(self):
        print("Sending an email notification.")

class SMSNotification:
    def send(self):
        print("Sending an SMS notification.")

# Usage
notification = NotificationFactory.create_notification("email")
notification.send()
```

3. Singleton Pattern: This pattern restricts the instantiation of a class to one object. It is useful for managing resources like database connections that should be shared across tests.

Example of Singleton Pattern:

```python
class DatabaseConnection:
    _instance = None

    @staticmethod
    def get_instance():
        if DatabaseConnection._instance is None:
            DatabaseConnection._instance = DatabaseConnection()
        return DatabaseConnection._instance

    def connect(self):
        return "Connecting to database"

# Usage
db = DatabaseConnection.get_instance()
print(db.connect())
```

Conclusion

Incorporating design patterns into test suite development significantly enhances the structure and effectiveness of testing procedures. Patterns such as the Page Object, Factory, and Singleton not only facilitate the management and scalability of test code but also ensure that test suites are well-prepared to adapt to changes in application specifications. These strategies are fundamental in modern software development environments where efficient, reliable testing is crucial.

Chapter Eight

High-Level Test Automation Strategy

Strategic Planning for Test Automation

A thorough strategic plan for test automation is vital for embedding automated practices into the software development lifecycle. This strategy functions as a detailed guide that enhances operational efficiency and sharpens the accuracy of testing methods. The initiation phase of this plan is critical, setting the stage for effective tool selection, seamless process integration, and adept management of organizational shifts.

Vision and Objectives

Creating a clear vision and specific objectives at the beginning of the automation process is critical. These should directly align with the organization's wider goals such as decreasing time to market, boosting product quality, or streamlining costs. For example, if the primary aim is to shorten the product release cycle, emphasis should be on speeding up the testing phases. It's crucial that these objectives are designed to be Specific, Measurable, Achievable, Relevant, and Time-bound (SMART) to guide the automation efforts effectively.

Assessment of Current Capabilities

Evaluating current testing capabilities is fundamental in pinpointing existing strengths and identifying areas ripe for automation enhancements. This includes:

- **Current Test Coverage**: Assessing which parts of the application are manually tested and the types of tests utilized (unit, integration, system).

- **Tool Efficacy**: Reviewing the performance and integration ease of existing tools, as well as their user-friendliness.

- **Team Skillsets**: Examining whether the team is technically equipped to embrace new tools and technologies.

- **Infrastructure and Resources**: Checking if the existing infrastructure is adequate to support automated testing efforts.

Constructing a visual representation that aligns test cases with application features can be effective in identifying areas most beneficial for automation.

Scope Definition

Defining the scope of automation involves selecting which tests to automate based on their potential impact and the required effort. Typically, tests that are high-value, frequently executed, and demand precise results are chosen. This process should include:

- **Risk-based Prioritization**: Prioritizing automation of tests that are essential for functionality or have high failure risks.

- **Repeatability**: Opting for tests that are consistent across various software iterations or versions.

- **Data Dependency**: Evaluating the setup complexity of test data and focusing on tests that utilize stable and reusable data.

This focused approach ensures that automation efforts are directed where they can have the most significant effect.

Tool Selection Framework

Choosing the right tools is fundamental to the success of the automation strategy. The selection should be driven by a comprehensive framework that assesses tools against specified criteria:

- **Compatibility**: Making sure the tool fits seamlessly with the existing technological framework.

- **Usability**: Assessing how user-friendly the tool is and the learning curve involved.

- **Scalability**: Ensuring the tool can handle increasing test demands and complexities.

- **Integration**: Evaluating the tool's ability to integrate with other critical systems, such as version control and bug-tracking software.

- **Support and Community**: Considering the support level from the vendor and the vibrancy of the tool's user community.

An objective tool evaluation can be facilitated through a weighted scoring model that quantitatively assesses each tool against these criteria:

Example Tool Evaluation Code

Below is a straightforward Python script designed to help in evaluating automation tools based on defined criteria:

```python
criteria = ['Compatibility', 'Usability', 'Scalability', 'Integration', 'Support']
weights = [0.20, 0.20, 0.20, 0.20, 0.20]  # Each criterion weighted equally
tools_scores = {
    'ToolA': [9, 7, 8, 6, 8],
    'ToolB': [7, 9, 7, 8, 9],
    'ToolC': [8, 6, 9, 7, 7]
}

def evaluate_tools(tools_scores, weights):
    scores = {}
    for tool, scores_list in tools_scores.items():
        total_score = sum(score * weight for score, weight in zip(scores_list, weights))
        scores[tool] = round(total_score, 2)
    return scores

# Calculate and display the scores for each tool
tool_evaluation = evaluate_tools(tools_scores, weights)
print(tool_evaluation)
```

Conclusion

Creating a strategic plan for test automation is a complex process that entails establishing clear objectives, analyzing the current testing environment, defining the scope of automation, and carefully selecting the right tools. Following these structured guidelines ensures that automation efforts are aligned with the strategic business objectives, preparing organizations for success in the fast-paced world of software development.

Selecting Tools and Frameworks at an Enterprise Level

Choosing appropriate tools and frameworks for test automation within an enterprise involves strategic planning and careful consideration. This decision significantly influences the effectiveness and efficiency of the software development lifecycle. As enterprises scale their operations and strive for enhanced software delivery, selecting the right tools and frameworks is crucial for sustaining robust and scalable testing processes.

Key Considerations for Selection

The selection process starts with a deep understanding of the enterprise's specific needs, which includes considering the type of software being developed (such as web, mobile, or desktop applications), the current IT infrastructure, the skills of the development and QA teams, and how well potential tools integrate with existing systems like CI/CD pipelines, version control, and issue tracking systems.

Compatibility Requirements

Tools and frameworks should seamlessly fit into the existing technological environment to avoid extensive modifications to current systems. This compatibility helps reduce the disruption typically associated with the adoption of new tools, thereby facilitating smoother transitions and quicker integration. For example, enterprises deeply integrated into a Microsoft environment might lean towards solutions like Visual Studio or TFS, which are designed to complement their existing setups.

Scalability and Performance

Tools must not only meet current needs but also scale with the enterprise. They should be capable of managing larger projects and heavier loads as the organization grows, without a drop in performance. It is advisable to conduct performance benchmark tests during the selection phase to verify that the tools can handle both current and projected demands.

Usability and Skill Alignment

The usability of a tool is critical. Tools with steep learning curves can slow down progress, whereas intuitive tools can significantly boost productivity. It's important to align tool selection with the team's existing skill sets or consider what training will be necessary to get the team proficient with new technologies.

Integration Capabilities

The ability of a tool to integrate with other systems is crucial for automating and optimizing development processes. Effective integration facilitates automated test executions, enhances issue tracking, and improves visibility and traceability across projects.

Vendor Support and Community Engagement

Strong vendor support and an active user community are invaluable when selecting tools. These resources are essential for troubleshooting and skill enhancement. Furthermore, the availability of additional resources such as plugins and integrations can extend the functionality of the tools and increase their adaptability to new challenges.

Evaluation Process for Tools and Frameworks

After establishing criteria, the evaluation of tools involves a detailed analysis and comparison of options. Many enterprises use a scoring system where tools are rated against each criterion, providing a quantitative basis for comparison.

Example: Tool Evaluation Matrix

Imagine an enterprise is evaluating three automation tools: ToolA, ToolB, and ToolC. They might utilize a matrix to score each tool based on criteria such as compatibility, scalability, usability, integration, and support. Here is an example implemented in Python, which could help in objectively scoring and comparing these tools:

```python
criteria_weights = {'Compatibility': 0.20, 'Scalability': 0.20, 'Usability': 0.20
    , 'Integration': 0.20, 'Support': 0.20}
tool_scores = {
    'ToolA': {'Compatibility': 8, 'Scalability': 9, 'Usability': 7, 'Integration'
        : 6, 'Support': 8},
    'ToolB': {'Compatibility': 9, 'Scalability': 7, 'Usability': 8, 'Integration'
        : 9, 'Support': 9},
    'ToolC': {'Compatibility': 7, 'Scalability': 8, 'Usability': 9, 'Integration'
        : 7, 'Support': 6}
}

def evaluate_tools(tool_scores, criteria_weights):
    final_scores = {}
    for tool, scores in tool_scores.items():
        total_score = sum(scores[criteria] * weight for criteria, weight in
            criteria_weights.items())
        final_scores[tool] = round(total_score, 2)
    return final_scores

# Display the calculated scores for each tool
evaluation_results = evaluate_tools(tool_scores, criteria_weights)
print(evaluation_results)
```

This Python script quantifies the evaluation, making it easier for decision-makers to choose the best tool based on pre-defined criteria.

Conclusion

The selection of automation tools and frameworks at the enterprise level is a critical and strategic choice that affects product quality, team agility, and the efficiency of the development process. Enterprises should adopt a systematic approach to this selection, ensuring the tools not only fit well with the current environment but are also scalable, easy to integrate, and supported by reliable vendors. By prioritizing these factors, enterprises can establish a testing environment that supports effective and sustainable automation.

Integrating Automation with DevOps Practices

Incorporating automation into DevOps practices is essential, significantly boosting operational efficiency, ensuring consistent outcomes, and minimizing human error across software development and operational tasks. As agile practices increasingly dominate to quicken development timelines, embedding automation within DevOps setups is becoming crucial. This synergy facilitates a seamless flow of continuous integration, testing, deployment, and delivery, thus speeding up release cycles and elevating the quality of the end products.

Significance of Automation in DevOps

DevOps blends the disciplines of software development and operations, aiming to unify these traditionally segmented roles to streamline the entire development lifecycle. This unified approach not only accelerates updates and feature releases but also ensures they are in line with business goals. At the core of DevOps, automation plays a vital role by mechanizing routine and complex tasks, enhancing both speed and accuracy.

Essentials of Continuous Integration and Deployment

Continuous Integration (CI) and Continuous Deployment (CD) are pillars of the DevOps philosophy, emphasizing the need for automation and ongoing monitoring throughout the app lifecycle. Key aspects of automation in CI/CD include:

- Automating the integration of code to ensure all changes are consistently and frequently incorporated into the main branch.

- Executing automated testing to validate that new modifications do not disrupt existing functionalities.

- Applying automated deployment techniques to ensure new versions are smoothly and reliably released into production with minimal human interaction.

These automated procedures are crucial for enabling quicker and more dependable software deployments, aligning closely with customer expectations and competitive market trends.

Essential DevOps Tools

Successful automation within DevOps relies on leveraging various tools that enhance these streamlined processes. Important tools include:

- **Jenkins**: This automation server helps manage different stages of the development pipeline.

- **Docker**: A containerization platform that isolates applications in containers, simplifying deployment and scaling.

- **Kubernetes**: An orchestration tool for managing containerized software, improving their deployment and operational efficiencies.

- **Ansible, Chef, Puppet**: These tools aid in configuration management, automating environment setups and maintenance across different stages.

Implementing Automation: A DevOps Use Case

Consider a scenario where a software team is establishing a CI/CD pipeline for a new project. The aim is to automate the processes from code commit to production deployment:

1. **Source Control**: Code is managed on a platform like GitHub.

2. **Automated Build**: Jenkins automatically initiates a build process upon each new code commit.

3. **Automated Testing**: After building, the application undergoes automated tests to ensure its integrity and performance.

4. **Automated Deployment**: Passing the tests triggers deployment to a staging environment using Ansible for precise environment configuration.

5. **Production Deployment**: Successful staging leads to final deployment in the production environment.

Here's a sample Jenkins pipeline script that automates these steps:

```
pipeline {
    agent any
    stages {
        stage('Build') {
            steps {
                script {
                    // Command to compile the project
                    sh 'make build'
                }
            }
        }
        stage('Test') {
            steps {
                script {
                    // Command to run automated tests
                    sh 'make test'
                }
            }
        }
```

```
stage('Deploy to Staging') {
    steps {
        script {
            // Use Ansible to deploy to a staging environment
            ansiblePlaybook(playbook: 'staging-setup.yml')
        }
    }
}
stage('Production') {
    steps {
        script {
            // Deploy to production using Ansible
            ansiblePlaybook(playbook: 'production-deploy.yml')
        }
    }
}
}
```

This Jenkins pipeline, scripted in Groovy, defines clear steps to automate the build, test, and deployment phases, demonstrating the integration of automation in DevOps.

Conclusion

Embedding automation within DevOps strategies revolutionizes the development, testing, and deployment phases, significantly enhancing deployment frequency, responsiveness to market changes, and overall software quality. When effectively implemented, automation ensures that the development processes are not only quicker but also more reliable, aligning perfectly with strategic business objectives.

Chapter Nine

Continuous Improvement Processes

Implementing Kaizen in QA

Adopting the Kaizen approach in Quality Assurance (QA) practices can significantly enhance the precision and efficiency of these processes. Kaizen, a Japanese philosophy that translates to "continuous improvement," promotes ongoing, small-scale enhancements that lead to significant overall improvements over time. In QA, this approach is particularly valuable for continuously refining procedures, reducing errors, and optimizing performance.

Insights into Kaizen in QA

The deployment of Kaizen within QA aims to continually improve the quality of outputs and the efficiency of QA operations through regular, minor updates. This strategy helps minimize inefficiencies, refine operational workflows, and boost the motivation and productivity of QA teams. Fundamental to the Kaizen philosophy are principles like teamwork, discipline, morale boosting, establishing quality circles, and fostering a culture of continuous feedback.

Core Practices of Kaizen in QA:

1. **Standardization**: Implementing uniform standards for recurring tasks ensures consistency and facilitates quicker identification of issues.

2. **Visualization**: Utilizing visual tools to map out and monitor processes and progress simplifies workflow comprehension and enhances monitoring efficiency.

3. **5S Methodology**: Adopting the 5S approach (Sort, Set in order, Shine, Standardize, Sustain) helps maintain an orderly and functional workspace, positively influencing productivity.

4. **Feedback Systems**: Developing consistent feedback mechanisms ensures that improvements are perpetual and that processes are adaptable to new challenges.

Steps for Implementing Kaizen in QA

To effectively integrate Kaizen within QA operations, a structured approach is recommended:

Step 1: Identify Improvement Opportunities

The first step involves pinpointing specific areas within QA that are ripe for improvement. This may include objectives such as reducing test cycle durations, lowering defect rates, or speeding up issue response times. Clearly articulated goals provide a direction for the continuous improvement efforts and establish a benchmark for assessing progress.

Step 2: Promote Team Collaboration

Kaizen works best when there is full participation from the entire team. Encouraging QA team members to contribute ideas and participate in identifying inefficiencies ensures a collaborative approach to the continuous improvement process.

Step 3: Conduct Training and Development

Offering training sessions on Kaizen principles and methodologies empowers team members with the necessary tools to actively engage in the improvement process. Training may cover areas like efficient problem-solving, the 5S methodology, and root cause analysis.

Step 4: Implement Supportive Technologies

Incorporating tools that align with Kaizen principles, such as Kanban boards for task management and software for detailed root cause analysis, helps in identifying and addressing inefficiencies effectively.

Example: Kaizen Blitz for Rapid Improvement

A Kaizen Blitz is a concentrated effort to address specific issues swiftly and effectively. In a QA context, this might mean focusing on rapidly reducing a backlog of defects.

Consider this example of a script for a tool that might facilitate a Kaizen Blitz aimed at quickly resolving defects:

```python
# Example Code for a Kaizen Blitz in QA

class Defect:
    def __init__(self, id, description, status):
        self.id = id
        self.description = description
        self.status = status  # New, In Progress, Resolved

def execute_kaizen_blitz(defects):
    for defect in defects:
        if defect.status == 'New':
            print(f"Initiating immediate action for defect {defect.id}.")
            defect.status = 'In Progress'
        elif defect.status == 'In Progress':
            print(f"Driving fast resolution for defect {defect.id}.")
        elif defect.status == 'Resolved':
            print(f"Closing out resolved defect {defect.id}.")
        else:
            raise ValueError("Invalid status encountered")

# Example Execution
defects = [Defect(1, 'API connectivity issue', 'New'), Defect(2, 'UI responsiveness problem', 'New')]
execute_kaizen_blitz(defects)
```

This pseudo-code demonstrates how a software tool could support a focused Kaizen Blitz in a QA setting, aiming for quick identification and resolution of defects.

Advantages of Kaizen in QA

The introduction of Kaizen into QA offers numerous benefits:

- **Superior Product Quality**: Continuous small enhancements substantially raise product quality.

- **Streamlined Processes**: Ongoing improvements make QA processes more efficient.

- **Enhanced Team Dynamics**: Engaging team members in the improvement process boosts morale and promotes a positive work environment.

- **Cost Reduction**: Improved process efficiency leads to reduced operational costs through better resource management and decreased waste.

Conclusion

Implementing Kaizen in QA not only fine-tunes operational processes but also establishes a proactive culture focused on continuous improvement. This approach ensures that QA teams are agile, effective, and closely aligned with broader business objectives, resulting in enhanced product quality and higher customer satisfaction. By diligently applying Kaizen principles, organizations can achieve notable gains in performance, driving greater overall success and customer contentment.

Techniques for Continuous Learning and Improvement

In the rapidly changing business environment, maintaining a commitment to continuous learning and improvement is crucial for staying competitive. This approach not only facilitates adaptation to new challenges but also promotes ongoing innovation. Here, we explore various strategies that can be employed by both individuals and organizations to nurture a culture of continuous learning and ongoing process enhancement.

Fundamentals of Continuous Learning and Improvement

Continuous learning involves perpetually expanding one's skills and knowledge base through diverse methods, aimed at both personal and professional growth. Continuous improvement, closely tied to practices such as Kaizen, focuses on making small, regular enhancements in products or processes, guided by thorough analysis and adjustments.

Strategies to Enhance Continuous Learning

1. Integrate Learning into Everyday Activities

Organizations that succeed in creating a learning culture make education a part of regular work routines. This could involve scheduling specific times for training within the workday or encouraging employees to dedicate a set amount of time each week to develop new skills.

Example: A software team could reserve the last hour of every Friday for workshops where they discuss new technologies or review current projects to identify potential improvements.

2. Utilize Modern Technologies

With today's technological advancements, numerous tools and platforms are available to facilitate ongoing learning. Organizations can leverage online educational platforms (like Coursera or LinkedIn Learning) to keep their teams knowledgeable about the latest industry trends and practices.

Setting up internal knowledge-sharing platforms can also promote a continuous exchange of information.

```python
import requests

def fetch_course_details(platform_url, course_identifier):
    response = requests.get(f"{platform_url}/courses/{course_identifier}")
    return response.json()

# Usage example
course_details = fetch_course_details("https://learninghub.com/api",
    "advanced_project_management")
print(course_details)
```

This Python script demonstrates how to programmatically retrieve educational content, which could be integrated into an internal company portal.

3. Foster a Culture of Constructive Feedback

Continuous learning thrives in environments where feedback is regularly exchanged. Companies should encourage a feedback-rich atmosphere by conducting frequent reviews and creating forums where peers can offer constructive criticism and suggestions for improvement.

4. Establish Incremental Learning Objectives

Setting clear, measurable goals can drive learning and improvement. These objectives should provide enough challenge to motivate and push individuals and teams beyond their current capabilities but remain attainable to prevent discouragement.

Example: Aim to decrease software deployment issues by 10% through enhanced QA testing protocols over the next six months.

Strategies for Continuous Process Improvement

1. Routine Process Reviews

Implementing regular evaluations of existing workflows and methodologies, such as through PDCA (Plan, Do, Check, Act) cycles, helps in continually refining operations.

2. Leverage Analytics and Metrics

Making decisions based on data is essential for effective improvements. Tracking performance metrics allows organizations to identify areas of inefficiency and address them systematically.

Example: Analyzing time tracking data to pinpoint where project bottlenecks are occurring.

3. Promote Interdepartmental Cooperation

Encouraging collaboration across various departments can lead to more comprehensive improvements. Diverse teams often find innovative solutions that might not be apparent when working within siloed groups.

4. Standardize Improvement Practices

For continuous improvement to become a staple within organizational culture, it should be formalized through regular skill-building workshops, training, and recognition programs that reward successful innovation and enhancements.

Conclusion

Adopting continuous learning and improvement strategies is essential for businesses and individuals aiming to thrive in today's dynamic market landscape. By implementing these approaches, organizations not only equip their workforce with the necessary tools to face future challenges but also enhance their overall agility and competitiveness. This proactive stance on personal and organizational development fosters a culture that values growth, adaptation, and sustained success.

Role of Feedback in Continuous Improvement

Feedback is a crucial element in the cycle of continuous improvement, acting as the driving force behind refining organizational processes and enhancing productivity. It enables companies to hone their practices and increase operational efficiency by providing essential insights into various aspects of their operations.

Significance of Feedback in Continuous Improvement

Rooted in methodologies like Lean and Kaizen, continuous improvement revolves around the PDCA (Plan-Do-Check-Act) model. Feedback is integral to this model, supplying the data needed to inform decision-making and evaluate the impact of changes made.

Structured Feedback Processes

An effective feedback mechanism is essential for sustained continuous improvement and involves several critical steps:

1. **Collection**: Systematically gathering input from varied sources such as direct employee feedback, customer evaluations, and performance metrics.

2. **Assessment**: Analyzing this feedback to uncover trends, problems, or areas ripe for enhancement.

3. **Action**: Implementing changes based on the analyzed feedback to improve systems or processes.

4. **Review**: Assessing the effectiveness of these changes to confirm they meet desired goals, thus completing the feedback loop.

This organized approach ensures feedback is not merely collected but is utilized to drive substantial improvements.

Types of Feedback in Continuous Improvement

Feedback within an organization can typically be categorized into:

- **Employee Feedback**: Insights from employees regarding their workflows, operational challenges, and suggestions for improvement.

- **Customer Feedback**: Reactions and satisfaction levels from customers pertaining to the company's products or services.

- **Process Feedback**: Operational data that assesses the efficacy and quality of current processes, often gathered through automated systems.

Gathering diverse types of feedback provides a holistic view of organizational performance and areas that require attention.

Effective Feedback Collection and Analysis Methods

Formalizing Feedback Channels

To maximize the utility of feedback, organizations should establish formal channels that facilitate regular and structured feedback collection. This might include digital feedback tools, periodic surveys, and interactive sessions.

Example of implementing a feedback mechanism in software:

```python
# Python function to solicit and record user feedback
def request_feedback(duration):
    if duration > 30:  # duration in minutes
        user_input = input("Please rate your experience from 1-5: ")
        log_feedback(user_input)

def log_feedback(input):
    with open('feedback_storage.txt', 'a') as file:
        file.write(f"User feedback recorded: {input}\n")
```

This Python code is an example of how software can incorporate a feedback prompt that activates after a user has interacted with the system for a predetermined period.

Analyzing Feedback for Insights

Analyzing feedback effectively is crucial for deriving actionable insights. Employing advanced data analysis tools can help organizations understand the implications of the feedback they receive.

For instance, using text analysis tools to evaluate customer feedback can help identify sentiment trends:

```python
import nltk
from nltk.sentiment import SentimentIntensityAnalyzer

def analyze_customer_feedback(text):
    sia = SentimentIntensityAnalyzer()
    sentiment_score = sia.polarity_scores(text)
    return sentiment_score

# Example execution
customer_opinion = "The new features are excellent and make navigation easier!"
feedback_sentiment = analyze_customer_feedback(customer_opinion)
print(f"Customer Sentiment Analysis: {feedback_sentiment}")
```

This snippet demonstrates how to apply the NLTK library for sentiment analysis, providing insights into customer attitudes towards a product or service.

Advantages of Effective Feedback Utilization

Incorporating feedback into continuous improvement strategies offers numerous benefits:

- **Improved Processes**: Direct feedback helps pinpoint specific areas for process enhancement.

- **Enhanced Employee Engagement**: Regular feedback mechanisms contribute to higher employee morale and motivation.

- **Superior Customer Experience**: Quick responses to customer feedback can improve satisfaction and loyalty.

- **Innovation Trigger**: Feedback often sparks ideas for innovation, leading to new initiatives or improvements.

Conclusion

Feedback is a foundational component of continuous improvement, facilitating the evolution of processes and ensuring alignment with strategic objectives. Through effective collection, analysis, and implementation of feedback, organizations can remain agile and responsive, continuously adapting to meet and exceed market demands and internal goals. This proactive approach to feedback integration not only drives efficiency and effectiveness but also fosters a culture of perpetual growth and learning.

Chapter Ten

Change Management in QA

Managing Change in Software Projects

Change management in software projects is a critical discipline that focuses on steering teams and technologies in response to new challenges and modifications in project scope, tools, or objectives. It involves detailed processes and methodologies to handle changes in a way that aligns with the project's ultimate goals and minimizes disruption.

Core Aspects of Change Management in Software Development

Change in software projects can stem from varied sources such as shifts in market trends, updates in technology, regulatory adjustments, or internal strategic decisions. Successfully managing these changes demands a systematic approach that ensures smooth integration and continued project progression.

Structured Approach to Managing Change

Effective change management in software projects encompasses several vital steps:

1. **Identification of Change**: Early detection and documentation of changes are crucial. This includes a

clear understanding of the change's implications, benefits, and potential risks.

2. **Analysis of Impact**: Conducting a thorough impact analysis to ascertain how the change will affect the project's scope, timeline, budget, and resources is essential. This step helps in deciding whether the change is beneficial and should be pursued.

3. **Approval Process**: Changes should be evaluated by a governance group, such as a Change Control Board (CCB), to determine their alignment with project goals. This body decides whether changes should be implemented, adjusted, or discarded.

4. **Implementation Strategy**: For approved changes, a detailed plan for execution needs to be developed. This includes updating project schedules, resources, and documentation, and clearly communicating these changes to all stakeholders.

5. **Review and Adjustment**: Post-implementation, it is crucial to monitor the effects of the change and evaluate if the desired outcomes are achieved. This might lead to further tweaks or additional changes.

Tools and Methods for Efficient Change Management

Communication Strategies

Effective communication is paramount in change management. Stakeholders need regular updates about the reasons for changes, the strategies for implementing them, and the expected results. Methods such as meetings, updates, and feedback channels are integral to a robust communication plan.

Embracing Agile Frameworks

Agile frameworks like Scrum or Kanban inherently accommodate change well, allowing for flexibility in project plans and easy incorporation of changes at various stages. Agile practices support a responsive development environment, ideal for adapting to change efficiently.

Example of managing tasks in an agile environment:

```python
# Simplified code to demonstrate task management in an agile software project

class AgileSprint:
    def __init__(self):
        self.tasks = []

    def add_task(self, description, status):
        self.tasks.append({'description': description, 'status': status})

    def remove_task(self, description):
        self.tasks = [task for task in self.tasks if task['description'] !=
            description]

# Instantiate a sprint
sprint = AgileSprint()

# Manage tasks
sprint.add_task("Refactor authentication system", "Pending")
sprint.add_task("Integrate third-party API", "In Progress")

# Adjusting to change by modifying tasks
sprint.remove_task("Refactor authentication system")
sprint.add_task("Implement OAuth", "Pending")

# Display current tasks
for task in sprint.tasks:
    print(f"Task: {task['description']}, Status: {task['status']}")
```

Utilizing Change Management Tools

Dedicated change management tools can significantly streamline the process of tracking and implementing changes. These tools often offer functionalities like change logs, status tracking, and impact reporting, which help in making informed decisions and maintaining project oversight.

Handling Human Factors

Beyond the technical aspects, effectively managing the human response to change is vital. This involves:

- **Training and Education**: Equip team members with the necessary skills and knowledge to adapt to new processes or technologies.

- **Involvement in Decision-Making**: Engaging team members in the change process can mitigate resistance and foster a sense of ownership.

- **Leadership in Change**: Strong leadership can guide teams through transitions effectively, providing clarity and support throughout the change process.

Conclusion

Managing change in software projects is a multifaceted challenge that requires balancing technical adjustments with team dynamics. By adopting a structured approach, leveraging agile methodologies, employing suitable tools, and emphasizing effective communication and leadership, organizations can manage change proficiently. This ensures that software projects are resilient, adaptable, and aligned with strategic objectives, facilitating sustained success and growth.

Ensuring Quality During Organizational Change

Preserving quality throughout periods of organizational change, whether triggered by strategic reorientation, mergers, technological upgrades, or acquisitions, is essential for maintaining a company's reputation and customer trust. This discussion focuses on methods to uphold high-quality standards despite the potential disruptions that come with change.

Integrating Quality Controls into Change Management

When organizations undergo transformation, maintaining quality can be challenging due to the potential disruption of established routines and the reallocation of resources. Implementing stringent quality controls within the framework of change management is vital to avoid deterioration in quality.

1. Defining Quality Objectives

Initiating any organizational change requires setting clear, measurable quality objectives that align with the company's broader strategic goals. These objectives should be communicated effectively across the organization to ensure all members understand and commit to maintaining these standards.

For instance, goals might include:

- Sustaining or improving customer satisfaction levels to at least 90%.

- Restricting product defects to a maximum of 2%.

- Guaranteeing that responses to customer inquiries occur within 24 hours throughout the period of change.

2. Ongoing Quality Evaluation

To identify and correct potential declines in quality promptly, it is crucial to establish mechanisms for constant quality assessment. This might include regular quality audits, continuous customer feedback mechanisms, and consistent performance assessments.

For example, in a software development setting, deploying automated testing regimes can help maintain quality assurance during updates:

```python
# Automated testing using pytest for Python projects
import pytest

def test_system_reliability():
    # Assuming a function 'system_check' should return 'pass'
    assert system_check() == 'pass', "System check did not pass."

# Execute tests to maintain quality standards
pytest.main()
```

This testing routine ensures that any modifications or enhancements to the software do not compromise the overall system reliability and performance.

3. Maintaining Transparent Communication

It is essential to keep all stakeholders informed about the quality objectives, the progress of the change process, and the strategies for addressing any issues that arise. Regular updates and the creation of feedback channels facilitate effective communication and collaborative problem-solving.

4. Supporting Training and Development

As new processes or technologies are adopted, providing comprehensive training and support ensures that all employees are prepared and can maintain quality standards during transitions. This support helps prevent a drop in performance due to unfamiliarity with new systems.

Utilizing Technology to Support Quality Assurance

Advances in technology can greatly assist in monitoring and maintaining quality during organizational changes. Data analytics, for instance, can provide critical insights into the effects of changes and guide further quality improvements.

```python
# Python script for analyzing key quality indicators
import pandas as pd

# Assuming data is captured in 'quality_metrics.csv'
data = pd.read_csv('quality_metrics.csv')
mean_quality = data['quality_score'].mean()
print(f"Average Quality Score: {mean_quality}")
```

This simple script allows for ongoing monitoring of quality scores, offering a clear view of how organizational changes impact quality metrics over time.

Cultivating a Culture that Values Quality

Creating and maintaining a culture that prioritizes high quality is crucial. Such a culture ensures that quality standards are upheld consistently, even in times of significant change.

Conclusion

Ensuring quality during times of organizational change is critical for any company that values its market position and customer relationships. By clearly defining quality objectives, continuously monitoring outcomes, facilitating open communication, providing necessary training, and utilizing technological tools, organizations can effectively manage transitions without sacrificing quality. These strategies not only help safeguard quality but also enhance the organization's capacity to adapt and thrive in new circumstances.

Tools and Strategies for Effective Change Management

For organizations aiming to navigate through changes efficiently while keeping a competitive edge, mastering change management is crucial. This involves utilizing a combination of sophisticated tools and strategic methods that assist in overseeing transitions smoothly, ensuring the organization's goals are achieved without significant disruptions. This article delves into the essential tools and strategies that are vital for adept change management.

Essential Tools for Change Management

1. **Change Management Platforms**: Systems like Prosci's ADKAR Model, ChangeScout, or Kotter's change framework offer structured approaches for managing transitions. These tools help in coordinating tasks, tracking developments, and maintaining uniform communication throughout the organization.

An example of how task automation can be implemented is shown below:

```python
# Python code for automated task distribution using change management concepts
import json

def assign_tasks(tasks, team):
    task_map = {}
    for i, task in enumerate(tasks):
        assignee = team[i % len(team)]
        task_map[assignee] = task
    return json.dumps(task_map, indent=4)

tasks_to_assign = ["Overhaul customer service protocols", "Conduct compliance training", "Deploy new software tools"]
team_members = ["Mike", "Angela", "Tyler"]
print(assign_tasks(tasks_to_assign, team_members))
```

This snippet illustrates an efficient way to allocate tasks among team members, streamlining operations and enhancing task management during change periods.

2. **Project Management Software**: Applications like Microsoft Project, Asana, and Trello are indispensable for managing the intricate details of change projects. They enable project managers to allocate tasks, establish deadlines, and track ongoing progress,

ensuring thorough management of all change-related activities.

3. **Communication Tools**: Effective communication is vital during change management. Tools such as Slack, Microsoft Teams, and Zoom facilitate essential communication and collaboration, keeping teams synchronized and well-informed about the change processes.

4. **Feedback Collection Tools**: It is essential to capture feedback efficiently during changes. Platforms like SurveyMonkey and Google Forms make it easy to collect and analyze feedback from various stakeholders, allowing organizations to adjust their change strategies dynamically and improve outcomes.

Strategic Approaches to Change Management

1. **Leadership Engagement**: The involvement of leadership is critical in driving successful change. Leaders need to actively support the transition, providing clear guidance and encouragement to all levels of the organization.

2. **Understanding Stakeholder Impacts**: Analyzing how changes affect various stakeholders allows for the creation of tailored strategies that facilitate smoother transitions and minimize resistance.

3. **Comprehensive Training and Support**: Adequate preparation through training and continuous support equips employees to handle new challenges introduced

by changes, ensuring operational continuity and reducing pushback.

4. **Encouraging Change Advocates**: Cultivating change advocates within the organization can significantly enhance the effectiveness of the change initiative. These individuals act as catalysts for change, promoting positive attitudes and encouraging adoption among their peers.

5. **Deciding on the Implementation Approach**: Whether changes are implemented incrementally or in a radical fashion can influence their success. Incremental changes often yield less disruption and resistance, whereas radical changes, although potentially more disruptive, can lead to quick, transformative results.

6. **Aligning with Organizational Culture**: Changes that align with the core values and practices of the organization are more likely to be successful. Ensuring that new initiatives resonate with existing cultural norms enhances acceptance and integration.

Conclusion

Effectively managing change requires a balanced approach that includes the use of advanced tools and thoughtful strategies. By leveraging robust change management software, fostering open communication, and strategically engaging with stakeholders, organizations can navigate transitions effectively. These practices ensure that businesses not only adapt to new challenges but also excel in a dynamic business environment, driving sustained growth and success.

Chapter Eleven

Quality Assurance Leadership

Leadership Skills for QA Professionals

Leadership within the Quality Assurance (QA) sector is crucial, transcending beyond mere testing to encompass a broad range of competencies that assure products not only meet but exceed the required standards of quality before reaching the consumer. As technological complexities increase, there is a growing need for proficient QA leaders who can adeptly handle challenges, lead quality-driven initiatives, and cultivate an environment of ongoing improvement. This article outlines the essential leadership skills required for QA professionals to effectively navigate their roles.

Strategic Insight and Analytical Acumen

At the core of proficient QA leadership lies the ability to strategically plan and analyze potential future obstacles. Leaders in this field must proactively identify possible quality issues and devise preemptive strategies to mitigate these before they manifest. Such strategic foresight not only maintains high product standards but also reduces potential expenditures related to delays and defects.

It's critical for QA leaders to establish and communicate clear, attainable quality objectives that resonate with the broader business aims. These guidelines help steer the QA team through complex projects and ensure coherent collaboration with diverse stakeholder groups.

Technical Mastery

In-depth technical knowledge is fundamental for any QA leader. Familiarity with the latest testing tools, methodologies, and technologies is imperative, as it influences decision-making processes and fosters respect from technical team members.

For instance, a strong grasp of automation tools such as Selenium is essential. Consider the following simple automated test script using Selenium WebDriver in Python, which reflects the level of technical proficiency expected:

```python
from selenium import webdriver

driver = webdriver.Chrome()
driver.get("http://www.example.com")

# Testing to confirm the correct homepage title
assert "Example Domain" in driver.title

driver.quit()
```

This example underscores how QA leaders employ automation to streamline testing processes, demonstrating a blend of coding skills and understanding of QA tools.

Effective Communication

Communication prowess is vital for QA leaders. They are tasked with elucidating the significance of stringent quality standards to diverse audiences within the organization. Leaders must also possess the ability to demystify complex technical details for non-technical stakeholders, aligning technical objectives with broader business strategies.

Problem-Solving and Quick Decision-Making

QA leadership frequently involves solving intricate problems. Exceptional problem-solving skills are necessary to diagnose issues swiftly, explore their root causes, and implement viable solutions. Moreover, the ability to make rapid and informed decisions regarding product releases plays a critical role in maintaining project schedules and meeting market expectations.

Adaptability to Change

With constant advancements in technology, QA leaders must remain adaptable, continuously updating their tactical approaches and embracing new tools and methodologies. This adaptability ensures that QA practices are aligned with cutting-edge industry standards and project requirements.

Team Development and Mentorship

Effective QA leadership goes beyond supervisory duties to include mentoring and nurturing team members. Leaders are responsible for creating an inclusive environment that promotes professional growth, continuous learning, and recognition, which are crucial for sustaining team morale and enhancing productivity.

Conclusion

Effective leadership in QA involves a comprehensive set of skills ranging from strategic planning and technical expertise to adept communication and mentorship. By developing these skills, QA professionals can ensure their teams not only uphold but advance the quality standards required in today's competitive marketplace. Successful QA leaders do not just oversee product testing; they are instrumental in shaping the trajectory of quality assurance practices within their organizations, driving both product excellence and innovative quality solutions.

Building and Leading QA Teams

Developing and managing a Quality Assurance (QA) team transcends typical management duties; it entails forming a group dedicated to ensuring that products consistently surpass quality benchmarks before market release. Effective QA leadership requires thorough planning, careful team selection, and fostering an atmosphere of continuous improvement. Here's how to effectively set up and manage a thriving QA team.

Setting Clear Objectives and Goals

The foundation of a strong QA team is clear objectives. Goals might include increasing software reliability, improving overall product quality, or minimizing bugs found after deployment. Clear objectives not only aid in recruitment but also serve as performance metrics for the team.

Recruiting the Right Talent

A QA team's success greatly depends on its members. Selecting individuals who possess the necessary technical skills along with soft skills such as communication and adaptability is crucial. Additionally, consider how well potential hires will integrate into the existing team and align with the organization's culture.

For example, using a Python script can streamline the candidate screening process based on specific skills:

```python
# Python script to assist in screening resumes for key qualifications
def filter_applicants(resumes, key_skills):
    selected_candidates = []
    for resume in resumes:
        if all(skill in resume['skills'] for skill in key_skills):
            selected_candidates.append(resume['name'])
    return selected_candidates

# Sample data
candidate_profiles = [
    {'name': 'John Smith', 'skills': ['Python', 'Selenium', 'Effective Communication']},
    {'name': 'Jane Roe', 'skills': ['Python', 'Adaptability']},
    {'name': 'Alice Jones', 'skills': ['Python', 'Selenium', 'Leadership']}
]

# Required skills for the QA role
necessary_skills = ['Python', 'Selenium', 'Effective Communication']

# Execute the screening
print(filter_applicants(candidate_profiles, necessary_skills))
```

This script efficiently identifies candidates who meet the essential technical and interpersonal skills required for the QA role, enhancing the recruitment process.

Training and Ongoing Development

Once the team is established, prioritize comprehensive training and continuous professional development. This should encompass specific technical training as well as encouragement for pursuing additional certifications and learning opportunities.

Promoting Collaboration

Effective collaboration is key to a successful QA team. Encourage open communication and regular interaction within the team and with other departments to quickly address issues and enhance the quality of the software.

Utilizing Appropriate Tools and Processes

The success of a QA team also depends on the tools and processes in place. Adopting advanced testing frameworks and automating repetitive tasks can increase efficiency and coverage. Implementing tools like JIRA for task management and Selenium for automated testing is crucial.

For example, integrating automated test suites using Selenium can be showcased with scripts that handle routine testing tasks, allowing the team to focus on more complex issues.

Leadership by Example

The leadership approach significantly impacts team dynamics and productivity. Leaders should consistently demonstrate a commitment to quality, tackle challenges promptly, and maintain transparency about the team's progress and obstacles.

Monitoring Performance and Feedback

Regular evaluation of the team's performance against established goals is crucial. Use key performance indicators such as defect detection rates and testing cycle times to measure effectiveness. Provide constructive feedback based on these evaluations to encourage continuous improvement and skill enhancement.

Fostering Innovation

Lastly, nurturing an environment that values innovation and continuous improvement can lead to significant enhancements in testing efficacy and team morale. Encourage team members to suggest new methods and explore innovative approaches to problem-solving.

Conclusion

Building and leading a QA team requires a strategic approach that encompasses more than just overseeing technical tasks; it involves inspiring a team, championing quality, and promoting growth and innovation. By carefully selecting team members, fostering a collaborative work environment, and continually investing in their development, you can direct a QA team that not only meets but exceeds the stringent quality standards required in today's competitive environment, thereby significantly contributing to the organization's success.

Strategic Decision-Making in QA

Strategic decision-making within Quality Assurance (QA) is pivotal for ensuring that QA initiatives closely align with the broader business goals, thereby enhancing product quality and contributing to organizational success. This requires decisions that influence project directions, resource management, and ultimately, the efficacy of the QA processes. Here, we delve into the essential aspects of strategic decision-making in QA settings.

Aligning QA with Business Objectives

QA functions must be intricately linked with organizational objectives. Strategic decisions in QA should bolster business aims such as reducing time-to-market, controlling costs, heightening customer satisfaction, and complying with regulatory standards. For instance, if accelerating market readiness is a priority, QA managers might opt to escalate investments in automation technologies to quicken testing phases.

Consider the following example, which uses Selenium for automating a web testing process to save time:

```python
from selenium import webdriver

def test_login_functionality():
    driver = webdriver.Chrome()
    driver.get("http://example.com/login")

    # Automating the login form process
    driver.find_element_by_id("username").send_keys("testuser")
    driver.find_element_by_id("password").send_keys("securepassword")
    driver.find_element_by_id("submit").click()

    # Verifying successful login
    welcome_message = driver.find_element_by_id("welcome").text
    assert "Welcome back, testuser!" in welcome_message

    driver.quit()

test_login_functionality()
```

This automated test verifies a login process, illustrating how automation can effectively reduce manual testing time and expedite overall QA processes.

Leveraging Data for Strategic Decisions

Informed decision-making in QA must be grounded in empirical data. Leaders should draw on data from previous projects to shape their strategic approaches. Metrics such as defect rates, test coverage, and bug resolution times are crucial for making informed choices. Analyzing these metrics helps uncover trends and pinpoint areas requiring attention or additional resources.

Here's a simple Python example to demonstrate analyzing test coverage data from a CSV file:

```python
import pandas as pd

def calculate_coverage(data_path):
    data = pd.read_csv(data_path)
    total_tests = len(data)
    passed_tests = len(data[data['Status'] == 'Passed'])
    coverage_ratio = (passed_tests / total_tests) * 100
    return coverage_ratio

# Assuming test data is stored in 'test_data.csv'
test_coverage = calculate_coverage('test_data.csv')
print(f"Overall Test Coverage: {test_coverage}%")
```

This script calculates the test coverage percentage, offering a straightforward metric to aid strategic decisions in QA.

Managing Risks Strategically

Risk management is an integral part of strategic decision-making in QA. It involves identifying potential software development risks and determining the most effective ways to mitigate them. Employing risk-based testing, which prioritizes testing in high-risk areas, is a strategic choice that can significantly influence the final product quality.

Communicating with Stakeholders

Effective communication of QA strategies and decisions to stakeholders, including project managers, developers, and upper management, is essential. This ensures that all parties are aligned with the QA goals and understand the strategic basis for certain QA actions, which promotes cohesive effort towards achieving common business objectives.

Conclusion

Strategic decision-making in QA involves a comprehensive approach that incorporates business alignment, data-driven strategies, risk management, and effective communication. By taking a strategic approach to these decisions, QA leaders can ensure that QA processes not only support but actively advance the business's competitive edge in the market. Implementing efficient tools like automated testing and utilizing data analytics to support decisions can transform QA from a supportive role to a central, strategic function within the company.

Chapter Twelve

Compliance and Standards

Understanding ISO Standards in QA

In Quality Assurance (QA), adherence to International Organization for Standardization (ISO) standards is crucial for guaranteeing product quality, increasing customer satisfaction, and ensuring compliance with international guidelines. ISO standards offer a set of protocols and frameworks that guide organizations in developing, implementing, and enhancing the efficacy of their quality management systems. This article explores the significance of ISO standards in QA, detailing their applications, advantages, and impacts.

The Role of ISO Standards in Enhancing Quality Assurance

ISO, an independent, non-governmental international organization, formulates standards that ensure the quality, safety, and efficiency of products, services, and systems across industries. In QA, ISO standards act as benchmarks for establishing a quality management system (QMS) that aligns with global best practices, adaptable to any organization regardless of size or industry.

ISO 9001, which focuses on quality management systems, is one of the most prominent standards in the QA sphere. It provides organizations with a structured yet flexible framework for managing quality throughout every aspect of a product lifecycle, from inception through to post-sale.

Key Aspects of ISO 9001 in QA

1. Customer Orientation: At the heart of ISO 9001 is the goal to enhance customer satisfaction by systematically fulfilling customer requirements and striving to exceed their expectations. Employing feedback mechanisms and conducting regular customer satisfaction evaluations are practical implementations of this focus.

2. Leadership Commitment: ISO 9001 emphasizes the importance of top management's commitment to the QMS. Leaders are encouraged to lead by example and foster an organizational culture where quality is a fundamental value.

3. Process Approach: ISO 9001 recommends managing activities as interrelated processes that function as a coherent system. This approach enhances efficiency and consistency through better resource control and process optimization.

4. Continual Improvement: A pivotal element of ISO 9001 is its emphasis on ongoing improvement of the system's overall performance. This involves making continual enhancements based on systematic and measured feedback.

Technical Implementation of ISO 9001

Implementing ISO standards into an organization's QA practices involves several technical steps. Here's an example of how a company might leverage software to track and enhance compliance with ISO 9001 through a simple Python tool designed to log quality incidents and monitor their resolution:

```python
import pandas as pd
from datetime import datetime

# Creating a DataFrame to log quality incidents
data = {
    'Date': [datetime.now().strftime("%Y-%m-%d %H:%M:%S")],
    'Incident': ['Error in product design'],
    'Status': ['Open'],
    'Resolution': ['']
}

df = pd.DataFrame(data)

def log_incident(incident_description):
    # Logging a new quality incident
    new_incident = {
        'Date': datetime.now().strftime("%Y-%m-%d %H:%M:%S"),
        'Incident': incident_description,
        'Status': 'Open',
        'Resolution': ''
    }
    global df
    df = df.append(new_incident, ignore_index=True)
    return df
```

```python
def resolve_incident(incident_index, resolution_details):
    # Resolving an existing incident
    df.at[incident_index, 'Status'] = 'Closed'
    df.at[incident_index, 'Resolution'] = resolution_details
    return df

# Example usage
df = log_incident("Discrepancy in software operation manual")
df = resolve_incident(0, "Manual updated and error corrected")
```

This example demonstrates how internal tools can facilitate adherence to ISO 9001 by systematically documenting and addressing quality issues, thereby supporting continuous improvement.

Advantages of Embracing ISO Standards in QA

Complying with ISO standards in QA offers numerous benefits:

- **Increased Customer Confidence:** Consistently meeting international standards can significantly boost customer trust and business reputation.

- **Operational Efficiency:** Standardizing processes usually results in decreased errors and less operational disruption, which can lower costs and improve performance.

- **Access to Global Markets:** Many global markets require ISO certification, so adhering to these standards can expand business opportunities worldwide.

Conclusion

ISO standards critically influence QA practices within organizations, offering frameworks that enhance product quality and customer satisfaction while streamlining operations. Though integrating these standards demands initial adaptation and effort, the long-term benefits, such as operational efficiency and expanded market access, are substantial. ISO 9001, in particular, provides robust guidelines that lead to significant business improvements and competitive advantages in global markets.

Compliance Issues in Software Testing

Ensuring that software testing adheres to legal, industry-specific, and corporate standards is critical for the successful market release of software products. Failing to meet these compliance standards can lead to serious consequences, such as legal penalties, security flaws, financial losses, and damage to reputation. This article explores critical compliance issues in software testing, outlines the primary challenges, and suggests strategies and technological solutions for effective compliance management.

Importance of Compliance in Software Testing

Compliance in software testing is necessary to ensure that software products meet external regulatory requirements and internal quality controls. This includes aligning with global standards like those from the International Organization for Standardization (ISO), adhering to specific regulatory frameworks such as the Health Insurance Portability and Accountability Act (HIPAA) for healthcare applications, the Payment Card Industry Data Security Standard (PCI DSS) for financial software, and the General Data Protection Regulation (GDPR) for software that processes data of EU residents.

Challenges in Compliance

1. Data Privacy and Security: Compliance with laws such as the GDPR requires that software testing includes rigorous validation of data handling practices to ensure data security and privacy.

2. Accessibility Standards: Testing for compliance with accessibility regulations such as the Web Content Accessibility

Guidelines (WCAG) is mandatory for software that will be used in public sectors or services, ensuring usability for people with disabilities.

3. Security Testing: Adhering to security compliance standards like ISO 27001 is vital for uncovering and mitigating vulnerabilities through in-depth security testing methods.

4. Third-Party Components: Software often uses third-party components, which must also comply with specific regulatory standards. Ensuring these components meet compliance requirements is essential to prevent legal and security issues.

Effective Compliance Management Strategies

Developing Compliance Checklists: Constructing detailed checklists that reflect regulatory demands can help ensure comprehensive testing coverage. These checklists guide the creation of test scenarios and aid in maintaining compliance documentation, crucial during audits.

Automating Compliance Testing: Automating certain aspects of compliance testing can improve accuracy and efficiency. Continuous testing for vulnerabilities and compliance drift can help maintain standards throughout the software lifecycle.

Regular Training and Updates: Keeping teams informed through continuous training on the latest compliance regulations is crucial. Knowledgeable teams can better implement the necessary compliance measures during testing.

Utilizing Specialized Compliance Tools: Incorporating tools that support static and dynamic application security testing (SAST and DAST) can facilitate the early detection of potential security issues. Compliance tracking tools can also assist in managing compliance documentation and processes.

Example of a Technical Compliance Solution

Here is how a Python script could be utilized to check for GDPR compliance in data encryption practices:

```python
import hashlib

def encrypt_data_compliantly(data):
    """Encrypt data using SHA-256 to meet GDPR compliance for secure data handling."""
    encrypted_output = hashlib.sha256(data.encode()).hexdigest()
    return encrypted_output

# Demonstration of use:
sample_data = "sample_data@example.com"
secure_encrypted_output = encrypt_data_compliantly(sample_data)
print(f"GDPR-compliant Encrypted Data: {secure_encrypted_output}")
```

This script showcases a basic implementation of SHA-256 encryption, a standard compliant with GDPR requirements for data security. This type of technical integration assists in aligning software testing practices with stringent data protection laws.

Conclusion

Navigating compliance issues in software testing is essential to avoid legal challenges, protect data integrity, and maintain user confidence. By employing rigorous testing standards, conducting regular compliance assessments, training staff, and using advanced technology tools, organizations can effectively address the complexities of compliance. As regulatory environments continue to evolve, maintaining a focus on comprehensive compliance practices in software testing becomes increasingly important, highlighting the necessity for proactive and detailed compliance management.

Preparing for Audits and Certifications

Audits and certifications are essential components in the software industry, serving to validate compliance with standards, bolster product integrity, and ensure that internal operations adhere to prescribed best practices. The preparation for these assessments involves comprehensive planning, detailed reviews, and stringent checks of all facets of software development and implementation. This article outlines effective strategies for preparing for audits and certifications, offering guidance on how to streamline these processes for success.

Overview of Audit and Certification Processes

The scope and nature of audits and certifications can vary widely based on the industry sector, the type of software in question, and the specific regulatory requirements involved. Common certifications include ISO 27001, which pertains to information security management systems, SOC 2, which deals with controls at a service organization relevant to security, availability, processing integrity, confidentiality, or privacy, and HIPAA compliance, crucial for software handling health information in the U.S. Each certification has distinct criteria focusing on evaluating a company's systems and operational procedures to ensure they meet established standards.

Essential Steps in Audit and Certification Preparation

1. Conducting a Gap Analysis: Initiate preparations by performing a gap analysis to identify where current operations do not meet the standards required for certification. This step involves a thorough assessment of existing practices, documentation, and systems to highlight deficiencies. Both internal audits or external consultants can facilitate this analysis effectively.

2. Enhancing Documentation: Documentation is crucial for audits and must accurately reflect current business processes in compliance with regulatory standards. It's vital to review and update all relevant documents, including policies, process manuals, and standard operating procedures (SOPs).

3. Employee Training and Engagement: A successful audit relies heavily on the staff being well-informed about the compliance standards and their specific responsibilities. Implementing comprehensive training sessions can equip employees with the necessary knowledge and motivation to adhere to stipulated practices.

4. Implementing Required Adjustments: Address any gaps identified in the initial analysis by making the necessary adjustments to processes, systems, or software functionalities. Managing these changes with minimal disruption and thorough documentation is crucial.

5. Conducting Pre-Audit Checks: Before the actual external audit, carry out an internal review to test the readiness of systems and staff. This mock audit can uncover any last-minute areas needing correction, ensuring the organization is fully prepared.

6. Fostering Continuous Improvement: Beyond passing an audit, maintaining ongoing compliance is crucial. Establish regular reviews and continuous monitoring mechanisms to sustain compliance as business processes evolve and expand.

Technical Insert: Automating Compliance Monitoring

Automation can significantly aid in maintaining continual compliance, particularly with routine checks and balances. Here is an example of a Python script designed to automate the verification of data security compliance:

```python
import hashlib
import os

def check_data_security(file_path):
    """Automatically verify the security integrity of a file by hashing and
        comparing it to a known good hash."""
    hasher = hashlib.sha256()
    with open(file_path, 'rb') as afile:
        buf = afile.read()
        hasher.update(buf)

    # This is a placeholder for the correct hash expected
    expected_hash = "YOUR_EXPECTED_HASH_HERE"
    current_hash = hasher.hexdigest()

    if current_hash == expected_hash:
        return True
    else:
        return False

# Path to the file to be checked
file_path = '/path/to/your/file'
# Execute the security check
if check_data_security(file_path):
    print("Data security is intact.")
else:
    print("Data security breach detected.")
```

This script exemplifies how to use hashing to ensure data integrity, a common requirement in several standards.

Automated scripts like these can be scheduled to run at regular intervals to ensure continuous compliance.

Conclusion

Preparing for audits and certifications requires a methodical approach involving detailed analysis, documentation revision, staff training, proactive adjustments, and continuous monitoring. By methodically addressing these elements, organizations can not only secure certifications but also enhance operational efficiency and quality. Leveraging technology and automation plays a pivotal role in this process, ensuring consistent adherence to compliance standards and improving preparation effectiveness.

Chapter Thirteen

Advanced Security Testing

Planning and Executing Security Tests

Security testing plays a pivotal role in ensuring software applications are safeguarded against potential threats and vulnerabilities. This vital phase not only identifies weak spots within the system but also verifies the software's ability to withstand malicious activities and protect sensitive data. This article will discuss a structured approach for effective planning and execution of security tests, including key strategies and a practical coding example to illustrate these concepts.

The Critical Role of Security Testing

The purpose of security testing is to expose vulnerabilities in a software system that could potentially be exploited and to devise appropriate defenses. Such testing is fundamental for maintaining data integrity, ensuring privacy, safeguarding user information, and complying with regulatory standards, thereby preserving customer trust and preventing potential legal consequences.

Methodical Approach to Security Testing

1. Defining Security Objectives: Start the process by establishing clear security objectives based on the specific needs of the application and potential security threats. Identifying which assets are most critical guides the focus of the security efforts effectively.

2. Performing a Risk Assessment: Conduct a detailed risk assessment to pinpoint the most vulnerable areas of the system and evaluate the impact of potential threats. This step is essential for prioritizing security measures and efficiently allocating resources.

3. Selection of Tools and Techniques: Choose the most suitable tools and techniques for the identified risks, which may include Static Application Security Testing (SAST), Dynamic Application Security Testing (DAST), penetration testing, and security audits, depending on the application's architecture and specific security needs.

4. Developing a Test Strategy: Formulate a comprehensive test strategy that specifies which tests will be conducted, the methodologies to be used, and who will perform them. This plan should also outline the resources required and establish a timeline for the testing phase.

5. Ensuring Adequate Resources: Make sure there are enough resources, including a team with the appropriate skills and the necessary tools, to carry out the planned security tests.

Execution of Security Tests

1. Setup of Testing Environment: Prepare a testing environment that closely resembles the production environment but is isolated to ensure that testing does not impact the actual operations or compromise data.

2. Implementation of Security Tests: Execute the tests as outlined in the test strategy. Automated tools can be used for extensive coverage, while manual testing may be more suitable for complex scenarios requiring deep analysis.

3. Detailed Monitoring and Documentation: Keep thorough records and monitor all aspects of the testing process. This documentation will be crucial for analyzing the test results and should be comprehensive enough to aid in diagnosing any issues encountered.

4. Analysis of Test Outcomes: Review the results from the security tests to identify any breaches or vulnerabilities. Assess the severity of these issues and prioritize their resolution based on the risk they pose.

5. Remediation and Verification: Address the identified security issues with corrective actions and conduct subsequent tests to ensure these vulnerabilities are fully resolved, confirming that no new problems have arisen.

Continuous Security Practice

Security testing should be an ongoing activity throughout the lifecycle of the software, continuously adapting to new threats and changing system configurations.

Technical Example: Security Header Inspection

Here is how a Python script can be utilized to verify essential security headers in a web application, which help mitigate various types of attacks:

```python
import requests

def check_security_headers(url):
    """Assesses the presence of essential security headers in a web application
    ."""
    response = requests.get(url)
    headers = response.headers
    required_headers = ['X-Frame-Options', 'X-XSS-Protection', 'Content-Security
        -Policy', 'X-Content-Type-Options']
    missing_headers = [header for header in required_headers if header not in
        headers]

    if missing_headers:
        print(f"Essential security headers absent: {missing_headers}")
    else:
        print("All required security headers are in place.")

# Testing a sample URL
sample_url = 'https://example.com'
check_security_headers(sample_url)
```

This script checks for the implementation of critical security headers, which are crucial for preventing clickjacking and cross-site scripting (XSS) attacks.

Conclusion

Planning and executing security tests require a well-thought-out strategy, meticulous execution, and ongoing adjustments based on evolving security landscapes. By adopting these systematic testing processes, organizations can significantly bolster their software's defenses, ensuring robust protection against both existing and emerging security threats. Regular updates to security practices and the integration of automated tools can further enhance the efficacy and reliability of security testing protocols.

Penetration Testing and Vulnerability Assessments

In the cybersecurity field, penetration testing and vulnerability assessments are vital activities that help secure an organization's information systems. These processes are crucial for identifying weaknesses that could potentially be exploited and for evaluating the effectiveness of current security measures. This discussion will delve into the basics of both approaches, outline their importance, and discuss how they work together to bolster cybersecurity.

Fundamentals of Penetration Testing

Penetration testing, or pen testing, involves simulating cyberattacks against your own computer systems to check for exploitable vulnerabilities. It's an active approach to discover security weaknesses.

1. Varieties of Penetration Testing:

- **External Testing:** Focuses on the assets visible on the internet, such as the web applications and servers, to determine what an outsider can access.

- **Internal Testing:** Assumes an insider attack starting from within the corporate network, useful for assessing how much damage a compromised insider could cause.

- **Blind Testing:** Gives the tester limited information before the test to simulate an attack by a typical external hacker without prior internal knowledge.

- **Double Blind Testing:** Increases the challenge by keeping security personnel unaware of the scheduled test, testing the effectiveness of the organization's security monitoring and incident response in real-time.

2. **Stages of Penetration Testing:**
   - **Planning and Reconnaissance:** Involves defining the scope and gathering intelligence like network and domain info to mimic potential attacker engagements.
   - **Scanning:** What systems are running, and how does the target react to various intrusion attempts?
   - **Gaining Access:** This stage involves web application attacks, SQL injections, and other methods to uncover vulnerabilities.
   - **Maintaining Access:** Tests whether the vulnerability can be used to gain a persistent presence on the target.
   - **Analysis:** This final phase involves compiling a report that details the vulnerabilities found, the data that could be accessed, and how long the tester was able to remain in the system undetected.

Fundamentals of Vulnerability Assessments

Vulnerability assessments are more passive than penetration tests and involve identifying, quantifying, and prioritizing (or ranking) the vulnerabilities in a system.

1. **Steps in Vulnerability Assessments:**

    - **Cataloging Assets and Capabilities:** Inventorying resources within the system, like hardware and software assets.

    - **Assigning Resource Value:** Determining the importance of different assets to the business.

    - **Identifying Vulnerabilities:** Scanning for known vulnerabilities that might impact each asset.

    - **Mitigating and Remediation:** Formulating a plan to address the vulnerabilities identified.

    - **Reporting:** Producing a report that details the vulnerabilities found, assessed risks, and recommended mitigations.

Integrating Penetration Testing and Vulnerability Assessments

While both penetration testing and vulnerability assessments can be effective separately, integrating them provides a comprehensive view of an organization's vulnerabilities. Penetration tests can confirm vulnerabilities found during assessments and help prioritize which ones to patch based on which can actually be exploited.

Example: Basic Network Scan Using Nmap

Here's how you might use Nmap, a network scanning tool, to conduct a simple scan that could be part of both a penetration test and a vulnerability assessment:

```
# Install Nmap on a Linux system
sudo apt-get install nmap

# Perform an Nmap scan
nmap -sV -p 1-65535 -T4 -A -v 192.168.1.1
```

This command performs a comprehensive scan, identifying services, versions, and operating systems running on the target, offering insights into potential vulnerabilities.

Conclusion

Regularly conducting penetration testing and vulnerability assessments is crucial for maintaining robust cybersecurity defenses. These tests help organizations identify vulnerabilities before they can be exploited by attackers, ensuring that protective measures are both effective and timely. By understanding and implementing these critical security practices, organizations can better protect themselves against emerging cybersecurity threats.

Ensuring Compliance with Security Standards

In the rapidly evolving landscape of cybersecurity, maintaining compliance with established security standards is not just a best practice—it's an imperative. As cyber threats intensify and regulatory frameworks expand, organizations are compelled to adopt strict methodologies that ensure compliance and protect critical digital assets. This section outlines a pragmatic approach to integrating security testing with well-known industry standards to foster uniform application of security measures.

Understanding Security Standards

Frameworks like ISO/IEC 27001, OWASP, and NIST offer structured approaches to information system security, each catering to specific operational needs or sector-specific demands. For example, ISO/IEC 27001 is geared towards improving an information security management system (ISMS), OWASP targets web application vulnerabilities, and NIST provides guidelines intended primarily for federal information systems but widely applicable in other contexts as well.

The choice of standards to follow usually depends on industry-specific requirements, the nature of the software in use, and operational geography. Compliance may be driven by legal requirements, customer expectations, or simply the necessity to maintain credibility and trust in a competitive market.

Integrating Standards into the Security Testing Lifecycle

To effectively integrate security standards into the security testing process, organizations must undertake several strategic actions:

1. **Gap Analysis:** Begin with a comprehensive analysis to identify how existing security practices measure up against the standards. This helps pinpoint vulnerabilities and prioritize their remediation.

2. **Security Control Implementation:** Implement the security measures identified during the gap analysis. These measures might include technical defenses such as encryption and firewall deployment, alongside

managerial policies like periodic security training and proactive incident management.

3. **Automated Compliance Checks:** To the extent possible, automate the monitoring of compliance. For instance, employing static application security testing (SAST) tools can automate the scanning of code to ensure it meets specified compliance standards.

```python
# Python script example for integrating SAST tools within CI/CD pipelines to
    automate compliance checks

import subprocess
import json

def run_sast_tool():
    try:
        # Execute the SAST tool and capture its output in JSON format
        result = subprocess.run(['sast-tool', 'scan', '--output', 'json'],
            capture_output=True, text=True)
        findings = json.loads(result.stdout)
        return findings
    except Exception as e:
        print(f"Error executing SAST tool: {str(e)}")
        return None
```

```python
def analyze_findings(findings):
    # Screen findings for compliance issues based on OWASP Top 10
    compliance_related = [f for f in findings if f['category'] in OWASP_TOP_10]
    if compliance_related:
        print("Detected compliance-related issues:")
        for issue in compliance_related:
            print(f"{issue['id']}: {issue['description']}")
    else:
        print("No compliance-related issues found.")

if __name__ == "__main__":
    findings = run_sast_tool()
    if findings:
        analyze_findings(findings)
```

4. **Continuous Monitoring and Testing:** Systematically test and retest security controls to ensure their effectiveness over time. Include regular security assessments and audits as part of this ongoing monitoring.

5. **Documentation and Reporting:** Meticulously document all compliance-related activities, such as test results, audits, incident management, and corrective measures. Create detailed compliance reports for internal stakeholders and regulatory bodies as needed.

Challenges and Best Practices

Ensuring compliance in dynamic tech environments poses significant challenges and requires a commitment to continual adjustment and improvement. Key best practices include:

- **Regular Training and Awareness:** Continuously educate both development and security teams on the latest in security protocols and compliance mandates.

- **Third-Party Audits:** Regular external audits can provide unbiased validations of compliance efforts and reveal hidden issues.

- **Technology Utilization:** Employ comprehensive governance, risk management, and compliance (GRC) systems to streamline compliance management.

By weaving security standards into daily operations and development cycles, organizations not only comply with legal and market demands but also enhance their defensive posture against a broad spectrum of cyber threats. This forward-thinking approach to compliance equips organizations to stay resilient and responsive to emerging threats and changes in compliance standards.

Chapter Fourteen

Future Trends in QA

Emerging Technologies and Their Impact on QA

Quality assurance (QA) is witnessing a paradigm shift, driven by the introduction and integration of emerging technologies. These innovations are enhancing both the efficiency and the precision of testing procedures, reshaping the conventional frameworks and strategies employed in QA. This overview highlights several pivotal technologies that are actively reshaping the QA domain, illustrating their capabilities and discussing the broader implications for the future of software testing.

Artificial Intelligence (AI) and Machine Learning (ML)

AI and ML are revolutionizing QA by moving away from traditional manual techniques towards automated, intelligent systems. These technologies significantly streamline testing by automating sophisticated decision-making processes and improving the detection of potential errors through predictive analytics. AI's capability to mine insights from historical testing data to anticipate potential defects is enhancing the focus and efficiency of testing strategies.

For example, consider the application of an ML model trained to predict potential test failures resulting from recent code modifications:

```python
# Example of utilizing ML to anticipate test failures due to code changes
from sklearn.ensemble import RandomForestClassifier
import pandas as pd

# Loading dataset that includes features like 'lines_of_code_changed', 'number_of_commits'
data = pd.read_csv('feature_change_data.csv')
features = data.drop('test_outcome', axis=1)
target = data['test_outcome']

# Establishing and training a random forest classifier
model = RandomForestClassifier(n_estimators=100, random_state=42)
model.fit(features, target)

# Applying the model to predict test outcomes for newly altered code
new_data = pd.read_csv('new_feature_changes.csv')
predictions = model.predict(new_data)
print(predictions)
```

Internet of Things (IoT)

The complexity of IoT amplifies QA challenges, as it connects a plethora of devices across varied operating systems and network conditions. Effective QA in this context demands extensive functional testing and advanced simulation tools capable of recreating diverse operational conditions to ensure seamless device interoperability and network reliability.

Blockchain Technology

Blockchain imposes distinct demands on QA, necessitating not only the validation of transactional integrity and data immutability but also the evaluation of system performance under various loads. This includes conducting thorough security examinations of smart contracts and assessing blockchain networks under simulated peak conditions to determine performance thresholds.

Cloud Computing

Cloud computing has transformed QA by offering scalable, flexible testing environments that lower barriers to infrastructure investment. This adaptability has revolutionized the integration of automated testing into continuous integration and deployment processes, providing ongoing feedback and facilitating rapid adjustments. Below is an example of how cloud environments integrate continuous testing in a CI/CD pipeline managed with Jenkins:

```
pipeline {
    agent any
    stages {
        stage('Build') {
            steps {
                sh 'make build'
            }
        }
        stage('Test') {
            steps {
                sh 'make test'
            }
        }
        stage('Deploy') {
            steps {
                sh 'make deploy'
            }
        }
    }
    post {
        always {
            junit 'reports/**/*.xml'
        }
    }
}
```

Augmented Reality (AR) and Virtual Reality (VR)

The advent of AR and VR introduces new testing complexities, necessitating QA strategies that encompass three-dimensional interactive environments. This involves developing testing protocols that accurately simulate user interactions within both augmented and virtual realities to ensure intuitive and effective user experiences.

Conclusion

As these emerging technologies mature, they promise to transform QA into a field characterized by greater automation, efficiency, and analytical depth. This shift not only enhances the quality of software products but also demands that QA professionals continually update their skills and adapt to these evolving tools and methodologies.

QA in Agile and DevOps Environments

In the realms of Agile and DevOps, Quality Assurance (QA) transcends its traditional role, embedding itself within every phase of the software development lifecycle. This approach promotes a seamless flow from development to deployment, significantly improving product quality and accelerating market readiness while nurturing a collaborative team environment.

Continuous Integration and Continuous Testing

Central to Agile and DevOps practices are Continuous Integration (CI) and Continuous Testing (CT). CI involves developers regularly merging their code changes into a central repository, which is immediately followed by automated builds and tests. This process ensures that integration issues are identified and addressed early, preventing them from compounding. The following is an example of how a Jenkins pipeline might be configured to facilitate this continuous process:

```
pipeline {
    agent any
    stages {
        stage('Build') {
            steps {
                // Build the application using the appropriate build script
                sh 'make build'
            }
        }
        stage('Test') {
            steps {
                // Run automated tests defined in the test script
                sh 'make test'
            }
        }
        stage('Deploy') {
            steps {
                // Automatically deploy to a staging environment
                sh 'make deploy'
            }
        }
    }
    post {
        always {
            // Archive test reports for later analysis
            junit 'reports/**/*.xml'
        }
    }
}
```

Shift-Left Testing

Shift-left testing is a strategy employed in Agile and DevOps to incorporate testing early and often in the software development cycle. By detecting defects earlier, it becomes easier and less costly to address them. This practice encourages developers to contribute to test processes through unit and integration tests, while QA engineers focus on developing robust automated acceptance tests that integrate seamlessly with continuous deployment workflows.

Collaboration and Communication

Agile and DevOps methodologies emphasize breaking down silos between departments, particularly between development, QA, and operations teams. This integration fosters a shared responsibility for the project's outcomes and leverages communication tools like Slack, Microsoft Teams, or JIRA to keep all team members informed and engaged, facilitating quick adjustments and decision-making.

Automation and Tool Integration

Automation is a cornerstone of Agile and DevOps, streamlining every step from code submission to deployment. Effective tool integration is essential, combining the capabilities of Git for source control, Jenkins for automation, Selenium for testing, and Ansible for deployment. Such integration supports a fluid and automated workflow that enhances both productivity and reliability.

Monitoring and Feedback

Continuous monitoring is critical in a DevOps setup, enabling teams to track the performance of applications in real-time. Utilizing monitoring tools such as Splunk, New Relic, or Datadog allows teams to gather actionable insights into application performance, which is essential for iterative improvement and ensuring user satisfaction.

Challenges and Best Practices

Challenges:

- Keeping test coverage comprehensive in rapidly evolving development environments.

- Scaling and maintaining the automation frameworks as projects grow.
- Balancing swift delivery with the imperative of maintaining high quality.

Best Practices:

- Foster an organizational culture that emphasizes quality at every stage.
- Regular training and development to keep team skills current with the latest QA practices.
- Constantly evaluate and refine QA strategies to adapt to project evolution and technological advancements.

QA in Agile and DevOps is an integral, ongoing, and dynamic component of software development, deeply influencing the quality and efficiency of the final product. By adopting these methodologies, companies can not only enhance their product quality but also bring their software to market faster and more effectively.

Predictions and Preparations for Future Challenges

Navigating an increasingly dynamic world requires organizations to anticipate and effectively prepare for upcoming challenges that span technological, environmental, and social dimensions. This analysis highlights the expected challenges within these areas and offers strategic approaches to mitigate and leverage these trends for organizational resilience and growth.

Technological Evolution and Associated Risks

1. Artificial Intelligence and Automation

The proliferation of artificial intelligence (AI) and automation technologies heralds significant shifts in the workforce, ethical dilemmas regarding autonomous systems, and heightened cybersecurity demands as AI integrates deeper into core business operations.

Organizations should respond by enhancing workforce training to pivot employee roles towards more complex, strategic functions that machines cannot easily replicate. Additionally, establishing robust ethical frameworks and decision-making transparency for AI operations is crucial. For example, companies can implement systems to log and review AI decisions, ensuring accountability:

```python
# Example script for tracking AI decision-making processes
import logging

logging.basicConfig(level=logging.INFO)

def evaluate_ai_decision(input_data):
    # Simulated decision-making logic
    decision = "approve"  # Example decision
    logging.info(f"Recorded AI Decision: {decision} for input: {input_data}")
    return decision

# Example of executing the AI decision-tracking
evaluate_ai_decision({"client_id": 400, "application_amount": 3200})
```

2. Quantum Computing

Quantum computing is expected to revolutionize areas such as data encryption and complex problem-solving. However, it may render traditional encryption methods obsolete, posing significant security risks.

To counteract these risks, entities should transition towards quantum-resistant encryption technologies and maintain vigilance on quantum computing advancements to adapt their security strategies promptly.

Addressing Environmental Challenges

1. Climate Change

Climate change presents profound threats to industries like agriculture, insurance, and coastal real estate due to its extensive and unpredictable impacts.

To fortify against these environmental risks, companies should integrate sustainability into their core strategic planning, improve infrastructure resilience, and utilize advanced data analytics for early detection and mitigation of potential climate disruptions:

```python
# Using data analysis to forecast climate change impacts
from sklearn.ensemble import RandomForestRegressor
import numpy as np

# Generating synthetic data for demonstration purposes
climate_variables = np.random.rand(100, 4)  # Four climate-related variables
financial_impacts = np.random.rand(100) * 200  # Projected financial impacts in thousands

# Machine learning model to predict financial impacts based on climate data
model = RandomForestRegressor(n_estimators=75)
model.fit(climate_variables, financial_impacts)

# Estimating financial impact from hypothetical new climate data
new_climate_scenario = np.random.rand(1, 4)
estimated_impact = model.predict(new_climate_scenario)
print(f"Estimated financial impact: ${estimated_impact[0]:.2f}K")
```

Societal and Economic Trends

1. Globalization vs. Localization

The tension between globalization and localization influences strategic decisions. While globalization offers expansive market reach and resource access, localization provides tailored responses and robustness against global disruptions.

Organizations can optimize their strategic positioning by blending globalization with localization efforts, ensuring flexibility and responsiveness to both global and local dynamics.

2. Changing Workforce Dynamics

The transformation in workforce dynamics, spurred by increasing demands for remote work, flexibility, and a balance between professional and personal life, calls for adaptive employment strategies.

Organizations should embrace these shifts by promoting flexible work policies, investing in technology that facilitates effective remote collaboration, and fostering a culture that supports diverse workforce needs. Continuous engagement and responsive adjustments based on employee feedback are essential to align workplace policies with evolving expectations.

Conclusion

Forecasting future challenges involves a nuanced understanding of ongoing trends across technological, environmental, and societal spheres. By strategically investing in innovative technologies, adopting sustainable practices, and being adaptable to changing social dynamics, organizations can effectively navigate the complexities of the future, ensuring sustainability and competitive advantage.

Chapter Fifteen

Case Studies and Real-World Applications

In-depth Analysis of Successful QA Strategies

Quality Assurance (QA) is critical in ensuring that software products not only align with user requirements and specifications but are also robust against failures when deployed. A strong QA strategy encompasses detailed planning, systematic execution, and iterative refinement, aiming to optimize both product quality and the efficiency of the development workflow. Below, we explore the key components that underpin effective QA strategies in contemporary software development environments.

Strategic Planning for Testing

A well-crafted test plan lays the foundation for successful QA. This plan outlines the testing goals, the extent of testing, resources involved, and timelines, serving as a guiding document for the QA team. Aligning this plan with the project's development methodology, whether Agile, Waterfall, or DevOps, ensures comprehensive coverage of all critical application areas.

Core Aspects of a Detailed Test Plan:

- **Objectives of Testing:** Defined goals that the QA efforts aim to accomplish.

- **Testing Scope:** Clear delineation of the areas to be tested and the depth of testing.

- **Resource Allocation:** Specifications of the personnel, tools, and environments needed for testing.

- **Timelines and Scheduling:** Detailed timelines for the execution of various testing phases.

- **Risk Management:** Identification and strategies for mitigating potential risks during the testing lifecycle.

Automation in QA

Incorporating automation within QA processes is crucial for enhancing test efficiency and breadth, particularly in repetitive and extensive testing scenarios. Automation frameworks like Selenium for web applications or QuickTest Professional (QTP) for desktop applications allow teams to execute predefined test cases automatically across different environments.

```
# Sample Selenium script for automating a basic functionality test
from selenium import webdriver

# Initialize the WebDriver for Chrome
driver = webdriver.Chrome()
driver.get("https://example.com/login")

# Input login information and submit the form
driver.find_element_by_id("username").send_keys("demo_user")
driver.find_element_by_id("password").send_keys("demo_pass")
driver.find_element_by_id("submit_button").click()

# Confirm the login was successful
assert "UserDashboard" in driver.title
driver.quit()
```

This example illustrates an automated test that checks the login functionality, ensuring that correct credentials lead to the appropriate dashboard.

Integration of Continuous Testing

Adopting continuous testing within Agile or DevOps CI/CD pipelines is fundamental. This involves setting up systems where code changes are continuously tested as they are integrated, ensuring the software remains bug-free at every stage. Tools like Jenkins or CircleCI automate these testing processes alongside development.

```
// Jenkins pipeline script example for a project's build, test, and deployment stages
pipeline {
    agent any
    stages {
        stage('Compile') {
            steps {
                sh 'make compile'
            }
        }
        stage('Unit Test') {
            steps {
                sh 'make unit-test'
            }
        }
        stage('Deploy') {
            steps {
                sh 'make deploy'
            }
        }
    }
    post {
        always {
            archiveArtifacts artifacts: 'bin/**/*.jar'
            junit 'reports/junit/*.xml'
        }
    }
}
```

This Jenkinsfile configuration illustrates a CI/CD pipeline that includes compilation, testing, and deployment, ensuring continuous integration and delivery of software products.

Focus on Performance and Security Testing

Comprehensive QA strategies extend beyond functional testing to include performance and security assessments. Tools like JMeter or LoadRunner help simulate user load to test application performance, while security testing tools assess vulnerability to potential threats.

Leveraging Metrics for QA Improvement

Successful QA strategies are reinforced by metrics-driven analysis. Performance indicators such as bug rates, test coverage, and cycle times provide insights that guide QA improvements. Regularly updating testing strategies based on these metrics ensures that QA processes remain effective and aligned with evolving project goals.

Conclusion

Effective QA strategies are marked by meticulous planning, integration of advanced automation, and ongoing adjustments based on performance metrics. By ensuring thorough testing, automating key processes, and continuously refining approaches, organizations can assure the delivery of high-quality software that meets both current and future demands.

Lessons Learned from QA Failures

In the realm of software development, Quality Assurance (QA) is fundamental in ensuring that applications not only fulfill specified requirements but also operate reliably under various conditions. However, QA processes are not infallible and failures do occur. These incidents provide crucial learning opportunities that can be instrumental in strengthening QA protocols. This discourse evaluates common QA pitfalls, distills essential lessons from these experiences, and suggests how to incorporate these insights into more effective QA frameworks.

Typical QA Pitfalls

1. Lack of Comprehensive Test Coverage

One frequent challenge in QA is failing to cover all aspects of the application, which can leave critical vulnerabilities unchecked. This often results from an incomplete analysis of the application's scope or failing to consider all user interaction possibilities.

Lesson Learned: Enhance test planning by conducting thorough risk evaluations and extensive user scenario analyses. Utilizing tools that measure code coverage can ensure all areas are tested, and continually updating test plans to accommodate new features and changes in user behavior is vital.

```python
# Example code for implementing code coverage in Python testing
import unittest
import coverage

cov = coverage.Coverage()
cov.start()

# Test suite for application functionalities
class AppFunctionalityTests(unittest.TestCase):
    def test_feature_1(self):
        # Implement test for feature 1
        pass

    def test_feature_2(self):
        # Implement test for feature 2
        pass

if __name__ == '__main__':
    unittest.main()
    cov.stop()
    cov.save()
    cov.report()
```

This script exemplifies integrating a coverage tool within a Python test suite to ensure all parts of the application are adequately tested.

2. Communication Gaps

QA failures are often exacerbated by inadequate communication between development teams, QA teams, and stakeholders, leading to a misalignment of expectations and objectives.

Lesson Learned: Improve communication and coordination among all parties involved in the software development lifecycle. Agile methodologies that emphasize daily interaction and regular updates, like daily stand-ups and sprint reviews, can help. Additionally, tools like JIRA for task tracking and Slack for daily communications can enhance transparency and collaboration.

3. Over-dependence on Automation

While automated testing is efficient for certain repetitive tasks, over-reliance can lead to issues that require human insight being overlooked.

Lesson Learned: Maintain a balanced approach to testing by valuing both automated and manual testing methods. While automation handles routine tasks, manual testing should be deployed for exploratory testing that assesses usability and complex user experiences.

4. Testing in Inaccurate Environments

Sometimes, the testing environment does not fully replicate the conditions of the production environment, leading to errors that only appear post-deployment.

Lesson Learned: Ensure that testing environments closely mimic production environments. This includes aligning configurations, databases, and any external integrations. Regular updates and checks on the testing environments are crucial to keep them aligned with production.

5. Neglecting Non-Functional Requirements

A common oversight in QA processes is focusing intensely on functional testing to the detriment of non-functional aspects like performance, security, and usability.

Lesson Learned: Expand the QA framework to include non-functional testing. This should involve using specific tools designed for performance testing like JMeter and conducting comprehensive security audits to ensure all bases are covered.

```
# Using Locust for performance testing
from locust import HttpUser, task

class UserBehavior(HttpUser):
    @task
    def main_page(self):
        self.client.get("/")

# This Locust test simulates user traffic to the main page, aiding in assessing
# how well the website handles concurrent users.
```

Conclusion

QA failures, while disruptive, offer valuable lessons that can significantly enhance the effectiveness of QA strategies. By analyzing these setbacks and incorporating learned lessons into QA frameworks, organizations can improve their assurance measures, ensuring the delivery of higher quality software. Ongoing refinement and adaptation to QA strategies based on past results are key to effectively meeting emerging challenges and technological advancements in the software industry.

Innovative Practices in QA

As software development continues to evolve rapidly, ensuring product quality through innovative Quality Assurance (QA) practices becomes increasingly vital. Modern QA methods not only address current testing needs but also anticipate future demands, integrating cutting-edge technologies and processes to maintain robustness and relevance. This discussion highlights several forward-thinking QA strategies that are transforming the landscape of software testing.

AI and Machine Learning Enhanced Automation

The integration of Artificial Intelligence (AI) and Machine Learning (ML) in QA automation is revolutionizing how tests are conducted and analyzed. These technologies enable predictive analytics, smarter test case prioritization, and dynamic test script generation based on real-time data.

Predictive Analytics for Test Prioritization: By analyzing historical data, ML models can predict which areas of the application are most likely to fail and prioritize those tests accordingly.

```python
import pandas as pd
from sklearn.ensemble import RandomForestClassifier
from sklearn.model_selection import train_test_split

# Example dataset
data = {'test_id': [1, 2, 3, 4, 5],
        'failures': [0, 1, 1, 0, 1],
        'execution_time': [10, 15, 10, 5, 20],
        'bug_severity': [2, 3, 2, 1, 3]}

df = pd.DataFrame(data)

# Features and labels
X = df[['failures', 'execution_time', 'bug_severity']]
y = df['failures']

# Split data
X_train, X_test, y_train, y_test = train_test_split(X, y, test_size=0.2,
    random_state=42)

# Model training
model = RandomForestClassifier()
model.fit(X_train, y_train)

# Predicting the likelihood of failures
predicted = model.predict(X_test)
print("Test Predictions:", predicted)
```

This example uses a RandomForestClassifier to analyze test data and prioritize which tests should be run based on historical failure rates and severity.

Integrating QA within CI/CD Pipelines

Modern software development benefits greatly from Continuous Integration/Continuous Deployment (CI/CD) methodologies. By embedding QA processes directly into these pipelines, teams ensure that every change is tested automatically, enhancing product quality and speed to deployment.

Automated QA in CI/CD: Integrating automated testing tools within CI/CD pipelines ensures continuous validation of code changes, with tools like Jenkins automating the execution of tests whenever new code is committed.

```
// Jenkins pipeline script example for integrating QA testing
pipeline {
    agent any
    stages {
        stage('Build') {
            steps {
                echo 'Building project...'
                sh 'make'
            }
        }
        stage('Test') {
            steps {
                echo 'Running tests...'
                sh 'make test'
            }
        }
        stage('Deploy') {
            steps {
                echo 'Deploying application...'
                sh 'make deploy'
            }
        }
    }

    post {
        success {
            echo 'Build and testing succeeded.'
            junit 'reports/**/*.xml'
        }
    }
}
```

This Jenkinsfile demonstrates how automated tests are integrated into a CI/CD pipeline, performing tests at every commit to ensure immediate feedback on the impact of changes.

Cloud-based Testing Platforms

The adoption of cloud-based testing platforms like BrowserStack and Sauce Labs enables QA teams to execute tests across a vast array of environments and devices without the need for extensive physical infrastructure. This approach offers scalability, diversity in testing environments, and cost-efficiency by leveraging cloud resources.

Real-Time Monitoring and Analytics

Post-deployment monitoring is crucial for modern applications, with real-time analytics tools providing immediate insights into performance and user interaction. Tools like New Relic or Datadog allow teams to monitor live applications and quickly rectify any issues that arise.

```python
# Example code for fetching real-time analytics from a monitoring tool
import requests

def fetch_app_metrics(app_id):
    response = requests.get(f"https://api.monitoringtool.com/apps/{app_id}/metrics")
    return response.json()

# Retrieve and display application metrics
metrics = fetch_app_metrics('app123')
print("Application Metrics:", metrics)
```

This script exemplifies how to retrieve and use real-time application metrics to monitor and ensure optimal performance.

Conclusion

Innovative QA practices are fundamental in driving the efficiency and effectiveness of software testing in the digital age. By leveraging AI and ML for enhanced test automation, integrating QA deeply within CI/CD pipelines, utilizing cloud platforms for flexible testing, and implementing real-time monitoring, organizations can not only improve their product quality but also adapt swiftly to changes and challenges in the software development landscape. As QA continues to evolve, these practices will become standard, pushing the boundaries of what teams can achieve in software delivery.

Conclusion

Summarizing Advanced Concepts

Summarizing complex technical concepts effectively is crucial for professionals across a range of technical disciplines. This skill facilitates clearer communication, enhances collaboration, and aids in explaining sophisticated topics to audiences that may lack a technical background. This article explores strategies for distilling complex technical content into accessible, concise summaries, providing practical examples to demonstrate these techniques.

Mastering the Basics

To accurately summarize an advanced concept, one must first thoroughly grasp its fundamental aspects. For example, understanding a complex algorithm in software development requires knowledge of its inputs, processes, outputs, and potential implications.

Essential Approaches:

1. **Decomposition:** Break the concept into its basic elements.

2. **Essential Element Identification:** Distinguish between the critical components necessary for a fundamental understanding and the more detailed aspects that can be streamlined for simplicity.

Communication Techniques for Clarity

Once the core elements are understood, the next step is communicating them effectively. This involves using straightforward language, incorporating visual aids, and employing analogies that resonate with common experiences.

Effective Techniques Include:

- **Simplification:** Use simpler language to convey complex ideas clearly without losing their technical validity.
- **Analogies:** Relate complex concepts to everyday experiences to make them more accessible.
- **Visual Tools:** Use diagrams, charts, and other graphical aids to visually represent information, which can often be more digestible than text descriptions.

Example: Machine Learning Simplified

Explaining machine learning to a non-technical audience should focus on overarching principles rather than granular details:

"Imagine teaching a child to recognize different types of fruit. You show them various fruits repeatedly, and over time, they start to recognize each type by its features. Similarly, a machine learning model learns from data. It is shown many examples and learns to recognize patterns, which it uses to make predictions."

```python
# Example Python script to demonstrate basic machine learning model training
from sklearn.datasets import load_iris
from sklearn.ensemble import RandomForestClassifier
from sklearn.model_selection import train_test_split

# Loading the dataset
data = load_iris()
X, y = data.data, data.target

# Splitting data for training and testing
X_train, X_test, y_train, y_test = train_test_split(X, y, test_size=0.3)

# Training the model
model = RandomForestClassifier(n_estimators=10)
model.fit(X_train, y_train)

# Calculating and displaying the model's accuracy
accuracy = model.score(X_test, y_test) * 100
print(f"Model Accuracy: {accuracy:.2f}%")
```

This code snippet provides an example of training a machine learning model, focusing on the process rather than intricate mathematical details, which is ideal for a summary aimed at a general audience.

Condensing Complex Information

When summarizing research findings or detailed technical specifications, focus on the results and their broader implications, rather than the complex methodologies employed.

- **Highlighting Implications:** Concentrate on what the research or specifications mean for the field or industry and their significance.

- **Audience Adaptation:** Tailor the complexity of the information and the technical terminology to the level of the audience's expertise.

Example: Summarizing Technical Documentation

When crafting summaries for technical documentation or research papers, it's important to offer an overview that covers the objectives, methodology, results, and conclusions in a manner that is accessible to non-experts.

Example Summary for Technical Documentation: "This report outlines the successful development and validation of a new encryption algorithm that enhances security by 35%. Our tests confirm that the new algorithm not only meets but exceeds current standards without compromising performance, indicating strong potential for widespread adoption in secure communications."

Conclusion

Summarizing advanced technical concepts effectively is a vital skill that improves with practice and attention to the needs of the intended audience. By focusing on the fundamental aspects, employing clear communication techniques, and adapting the message for the audience, technical professionals can ensure that their complex ideas are well-understood and appreciated by both their peers and non-technical stakeholders. This fosters improved decision-making and collaboration across diverse fields.

Encouragement for Ongoing Professional Development

In the dynamic realms of modern industries, particularly those driven by technological advancements, ongoing professional development is essential. This continuous learning ensures that both individuals and organizations remain at the forefront of innovation and market relevance. This article explores why professional development is critical, offers strategies for fostering a culture of learning, and provides actionable tips for professionals intent on enhancing their skills.

The Necessity of Continuous Learning

In fields characterized by rapid technological growth such as IT, engineering, and digital marketing, skills can quickly become outdated. Ongoing professional development is crucial for maintaining the efficacy and relevance of one's skill set, which in turn supports career growth and adaptability in fluctuating markets.

Advantages of Continued Learning:

- **Flexibility:** Keeping pace with industry changes makes professionals and businesses more adaptable and prepared for future trends.

- **Competitive Edge:** Continuously updated skills lead to innovation and efficiency, driving both personal and organizational success.

- **Enhanced Engagement:** Regular learning and development can mitigate job stagnation and boost career satisfaction, opening up new pathways and opportunities.

Promoting a Learning-Focused Culture

Organizations have a significant role in nurturing an environment that prioritizes and values continuous learning.

Such a culture not only supports employee growth but also enhances the organization's overall adaptability and competitiveness.

Methods to Encourage Continuous Learning:

- **Provide Learning Resources:** Offer access to educational tools, online course subscriptions, and internal training opportunities. Utilize platforms like Pluralsight, LinkedIn Learning, or specific trade-focused educational resources.

- **Establish Mentorship Programs:** Develop mentorship arrangements where experienced professionals can share knowledge and guidance with newer team members, enriching the organization's knowledge base.

- **Incentivize Learning:** Implement systems to acknowledge and reward learning achievements, such as providing bonuses, promotions, or public recognition for educational accomplishments.

Effective Personal Development Strategies

For individual professionals, engaging proactively in professional development requires thoughtful planning and commitment. Below are strategies to help cultivate and maintain professional growth:

1. Establish Clear Goals Set specific, measurable, achievable, relevant, and time-sensitive (SMART) goals that reflect one's professional aspirations. Defining what skills to acquire and the timeline for learning them provides a structured approach to professional growth.

Example Goal: "Master JavaScript and its major frameworks within the next year to transition into a full-stack development role."

2. Conduct Regular Skills Audits Periodically evaluate your own skill set to identify areas for improvement or updating. Tools like personal development plans (PDPs) can be instrumental in mapping out your learning journey and measuring progress.

3. Dedicate Time for Learning Allocate regular time each week to engage in educational activities. Consistent dedication is key to achieving substantial skill enhancement.

4. Engage with Professional Communities Active participation in professional networks can provide insights into industry trends and access to additional resources such as seminars, workshops, and conferences.

5. Practical Application of New Skills Integrate new knowledge into practical projects at work or through personal endeavors. This application solidifies learning and demonstrates the real-world value of new skills.

```python
# Example Python code for a beginner's project on data visualization
import matplotlib.pyplot as plt
import pandas as pd

# Load and visualize data
data = pd.read_csv('sales_data.csv')
plt.figure(figsize=(10,5))
plt.bar(data['Month'], data['Sales'])
plt.xlabel('Month')
plt.ylabel('Sales')
plt.title('Monthly Sales Data Visualization')
plt.show()

# This script helps beginners in data science to visualize sales data, applying
    basic Python skills in a practical context.
```

Conclusion

Encouraging ongoing professional development is crucial in today's ever-evolving professional environments. By fostering a culture that values continual learning and providing individuals with the resources and support needed for growth, organizations enhance their resilience and innovation capacity. For professionals, regularly engaging in developmental activities and applying new knowledge practically ensures continued relevance and career advancement in an increasingly competitive world.

Final Thoughts on Leadership and Innovation in QA

In the ever-changing world of Quality Assurance (QA), the integration of effective leadership and continuous innovation is paramount. As the technological landscape shifts and consumer demands evolve, so must the methodologies governing QA. This critical function benefits immensely from leaders who not only manage but inspire, fostering environments that champion exacting quality standards and encourage innovative testing methods. This exploration delves into how leadership and innovation are essential for the evolution of QA practices, impacting team functionality and overall process efficacy.

Influential Leadership in QA

Leadership within QA goes beyond the traditional scope of managing tasks and personnel. It involves cultivating a culture that values precision, promotes problem-solving innovation, and supports taking calculated risks to advance quality standards. Effective QA leaders are pivotal in initiating transformative changes, encouraging cross-functional collaboration, and embedding quality-centric principles throughout the product development lifecycle.

Core Qualities of Effective QA Leadership:

- **Visionary Leadership:** It is crucial for QA leaders to possess a clear and strategic vision that aligns the QA operations with broader business objectives, motivating the team to contribute to overarching goals.

- **Empowerment:** By empowering QA professionals to make impactful decisions and take charge of their workflows, leaders enhance team autonomy and initiative, which are vital for a dynamic QA environment.

- **Adaptability:** With the rapid technological advancements impacting every industry, QA leaders must continuously adapt their strategies and practices to stay ahead of industry trends and incorporate emerging technologies effectively.

Innovation as a Catalyst in QA

Innovation in QA extends beyond merely adopting new tools; it requires a cultural shift towards ongoing improvement and adapting practices to meet new challenges. By embracing innovative approaches, QA teams can improve their operational efficiency, derive more profound insights from quality data, and increase the overall value delivered to customers.

Strategies for Advancing QA through Innovation:

- **Adopting Advanced Technologies:** Integrating modern technologies like AI and machine learning can transform QA by automating complex tests and enhancing the ability to predict and mitigate potential issues before they manifest.

```python
# Example: Utilizing machine learning for enhanced QA predictions
from sklearn.ensemble import RandomForestClassifier
from sklearn.datasets import make_classification
from sklearn.model_selection import train_test_split

# Generating synthetic data for testing
X, y = make_classification(n_samples=100, n_features=4, random_state=42)
X_train, X_test, y_train, y_test = train_test_split(X, y, test_size=0.25, random_state=42)

# Training a model to anticipate quality issues
model = RandomForestClassifier()
model.fit(X_train, y_train)

# Predicting and outputting potential issues
predictions = model.predict(X_test)
print("Anticipated quality issues:", predictions)
```

- **Implementing Agile QA Practices:** By adopting agile methodologies, QA becomes more intertwined with continuous development processes, enhancing the agility and responsiveness of testing cycles.

- **Cultivating Experimental Mindsets:** Promoting an experimental ethos within QA teams encourages creativity and can lead to significant breakthroughs in testing and process optimization.

The Convergence of Leadership and Innovation

When leadership and innovation are effectively aligned within QA, the result is a significant enhancement in both the quality of outputs and the efficiency of processes. Teams led by visionary individuals who advocate for and implement innovative solutions are better equipped to proactively address challenges and deliver high-quality products that meet or surpass customer expectations.

Conclusion

In conclusion, leadership and innovation are indispensable to the contemporary evolution of QA practices. Leaders who foster an environment conducive to innovation empower QA teams to go beyond mere compliance, transforming them into proactive, integral participants in the development process. This forward-thinking approach not only elevates the capabilities of QA teams but also strategically positions organizations for enduring success and a competitive edge in their markets.

www.ingramcontent.com/pod-product-compliance
Lightning Source LLC
Chambersburg PA
CBHW071918210526
45479CB00002B/462